The Wreckwalker's Guide to the Coast Path from Erme to Dart.

Shipwrecks of The South Hams

by

KENDALL McDONALD

Although reasonable care has been taken in preparing this guide, the author and publisher accept no responsibility or liability for any errors, omissions or alterations, or for any consequences ensuing upon the use of, or reliance upon, any information contained herein. Due caution should be exercised by anyone visiting any site herein described or indicated. The reproduction by any means in whole or part of any content of this book is expressly forbidden without permission of the author.

Maps, by Wayne Acourt, are not to scale.
Front cover photograph by Frank Allen of the
Demetrios on Prawle Point in 1992.

First published 1996. Second edition 1998
Published by Wreckwalker Books, Cradles Cottage, Thurlestone,
Kingsbridge, Devon TQ7 3NE.
Copyright: Kendall McDonald, 1996
ISBN 0952863707

Printed by E.J. Rickard Ltd. of Plymouth.

WARNING: LEAVING THE PATH TO TRY TO PEER OVER OR CLIMBING DOWN FOR A BETTER VIEW IS VERY DANGEROUS. CLIFF EDGES CRUMBLE WITHOUT WARNING AND THE GRASS ON SLOPES LEADING TO THE CLIFF FACE CAN BE AS SLIPPERY AS ICE. CARE MUST BE TAKEN AT ALL TIMES WHEN WALKING BY THE SEA.

The Wreck Walkers...

CAN you imagine crowds of 10,000 people at a time walking along the route of today's coastal path? In the long ago so many people hurried to the scene of a shipwreck that they turned the path along the cliff tops into an earth road with their feet and cart wheels.

If you can't picture those scenes, you should have seen what happened only a few years ago when a modern steamer crashed into the cliffs of Prawle. An earth road appeared in next to no time when more than ten thousand people crossed the fields to see that wreck!

That modern wreck, and seventy much older ones, are all detailed in this Wreckwalker's Guide. Here are the stories of all the important shipwrecks of the South Hams, including some whose names we do not know, but whose graves lie close to the 40 miles of Heritage Coast Path bordering the South Hams coastline.

Shipping in every century has come to grief on the coast of the South Hams, which is the name given to the land between the Erme and the Dart and backed by Dartmoor. In summer this is a soft and gentle countryside, much loved by holidaymakers, providing them with some of the most magnificent coast-walking country in Britain. In winter, particularly in the days of sail, it was an iron shore, unforgiving of any mistake.

The only Spanish Armada ship wrecked in England, the *St Peter the Great,* ended up in Hope Cove trapped by on-shore winds. Nearly two centuries later *HMS Ramillies* was crushed to death close by. Her wrecking was one of the greatest disasters in the history of the Royal Navy. She was smashed to pieces on the cliffs of the Bolt with the loss of over 700 men.

The world's first shipwreck of an oil-tanker happened here giving the clear waters of Devon an unenviable first - the first sea in the world to suffer the misery of large-scale oil pollution.

Wreck followed wreck, sometimes with only hours between them. At Prawle Point, Devon's most southerly tip, there are at least seven wrecks close together. One is right on top of another and three are lying side by side with a fourth across the top of them!

The U-boats of both world wars hunted in these waters and sent more shipping to the bottom with a heavy loss of life.

A Q-ship, after an action which won its commander the V.C., is close inshore.

The Albert Medal was created because of bravery at one South Hams wreck. Two more Albert Medals were awarded after yet another wreck along the coast.

The accounts of these shipwrecks let us look through a window into the past. They tell us about the sailors' struggle to survive. But they also tell us of the living conditions which drove those thousands along the coastal path years ago, to watch and wait, and sometimes even to hope, for yet another ship ashore.

KENDALL McDONALD.

Foot Note: With this book, walkers should use a large scale ordnance survey map such as the Outdoor Leisure 20 South Devon - Brixham to Newton Ferrers (1: 25000; two-and-a-half inches to one mile), which names all the bays and coves of the wreck sites in this book. It also shows parking for those who want to go shipwreck-spotting, but not walk too far.

SECTION ONE –
ERME MOUTH TO BURGH ISLAND.

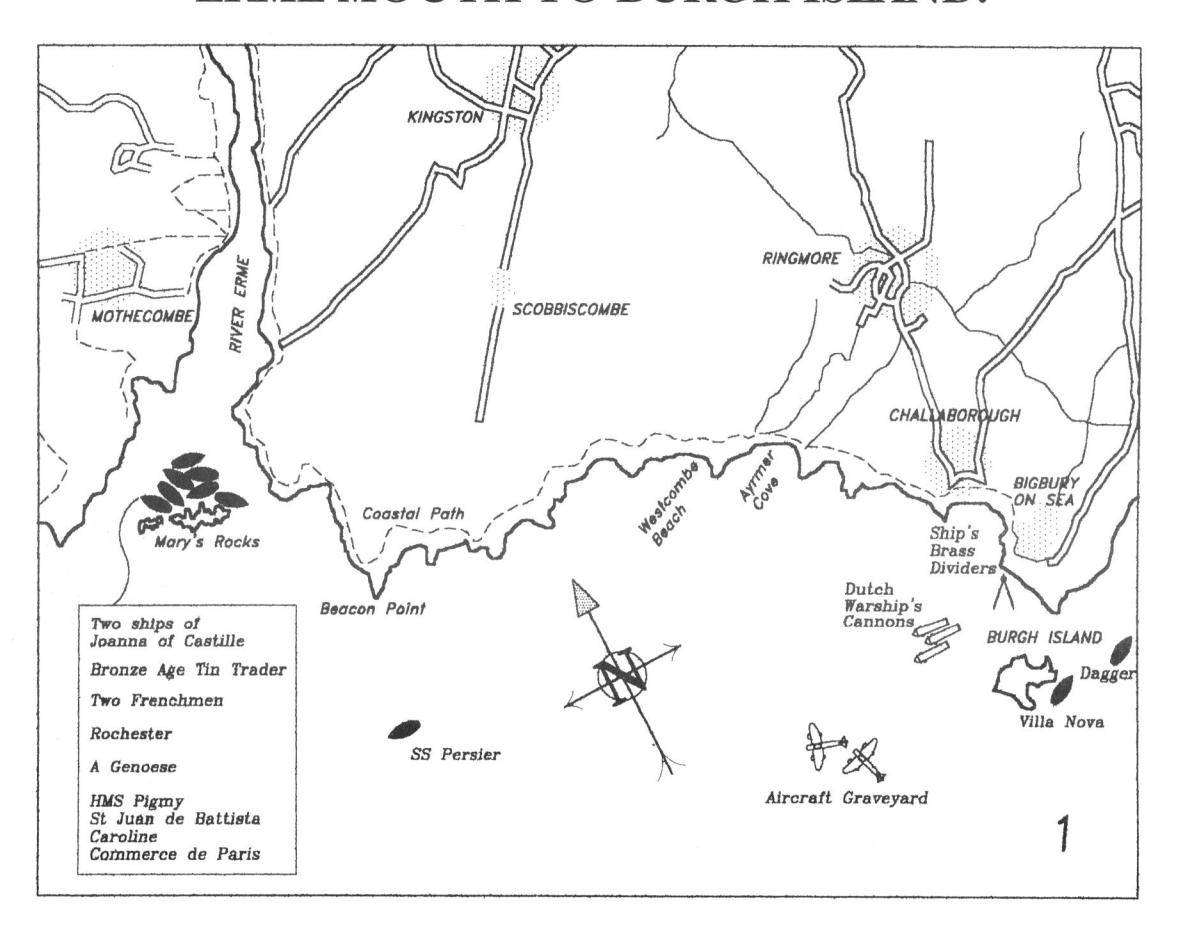

1. MAD JOANNA'S SHIPS.
The Erme. 1506

WAS Joanna really mad? Or was the fact that she took the corpse of her late husband, Philip the Handsome, with her whenever she visited castles in Spain powerful evidence of one of the greatest love stories of the 16th century?

Whichever theory takes your fancy, there is no doubt that two of Joanna's ships lie underwater at the mouth of the River Erme.

Joanna was the daughter of Queen Isabella of Spain and at the end of the year of 1505, she was in Holland, having just married Archduke Philip of Flanders. This may have been an arranged marriage for Philip, but for Joanna it was the culmination of her wildest dreams. She was madly, deeply, truly, in love with the man known in all the courts of Europe as "Philip the Handsome" and now her husband.

Then, suddenly, Queen Isabella of Spain died. When the news reached the court in Flanders, there was a fearful panic. Philip, by his marriage to Joanna, was now King of Castile with Joanna as his queen. There was no time to lose - an absent King could easily be overthrown. So on January 7, 1506, Philip and Joanna set sail to claim their kingdom with a retinue of 2,000 in a fleet of 300 ships.

On January 16 while in the Channel, the fleet ran into a ferocious south-westerly gale. The storm was so big that it is recorded in documents of the time as "a tempest". Philip's fleet was scattered all along the English coast and two of them were driven on to rocks in the Erme mouth. Philip and Joanna were not aboard these ships. Their much bigger vessels were forced to seek shelter in Weymouth.

It is likely that the ships lost in the Erme were more transports, than treasure ships. The first reference to the wreck site comes in the "Itinerary", written by John Leland, the Keeper of Henry VIII's Libraries, during a horseback tour he made of South Devon in 1535. He stressed what a trap the Erme Mouth was for the unwary ship when he wrote: *"The mouth of this lyith ful of flattes and rokkes and no ship cummith in tempest hither, but in desperation. Too of Philip King of Castelle shippes felle to wrak in this haven when he was dryven into England by tempeste"*. If they had been treasure ships, it would have been important enough for Leland to note it, but he didn't, and didn't mention the ships again.

In fact, we know that Philip and Joanna stayed in England - were almost prisoners of Henry VII - until March before setting off once again for Spain. Philip didn't last long after that. Within six months of returning to Spain, he was dead and Joanna went crazy with grief. She refused to allow him to be buried and took his body with her whenever she visited any other part of her kingdom. She was not a popular visitor with the landed gentry!

In recent years many divers have tried to find the remains of the ships of Philip and Joanna. None had any success until in 1990, Stephen George of Slapton, near Torcross, was snorkelling in the estuary when he spotted an extremely old cannon on the sandy seabed. Stephen George is something of a legend among divers in the South-West because of his ability to spot ancient items underwater. He reported his cannon find to Neville Oldham, chairman of the local section of the Nautical Archaeology Society, who put together a diving team to survey the area. They soon found four more large cannon, a large anchor, and a swivel gun still loaded with small stones instead of iron shot and held in place by an intact tampion in the muzzle. Amazingly preserved on the breech handle was a decorative rope knot. The swivel gun was dated by Austin C.Carpenter, one of the world's leading cannon experts, who lives in the South Hams, as made between 1490 and 1550.

There seems little doubt that this swivel gun, known at the time as a "murderer", was once mounted on the poop rail of one of Joanna's ships. The swivel guns were used for close-quarter fighting, for spraying the enemy's decks or swivelling round to sweep your own if you had been boarded.

The divers' next discovery gave them quite a shock. One of the other guns was positively identified as a Swedish-made finbanker cannon of 1690-1705! To add to their confusion their next find was a French half-ecu coin dated 1621. Then a lead pan weight stamped with the mark of Guildhall in London and the French mark of St.Lo used between 1549 and 1780.

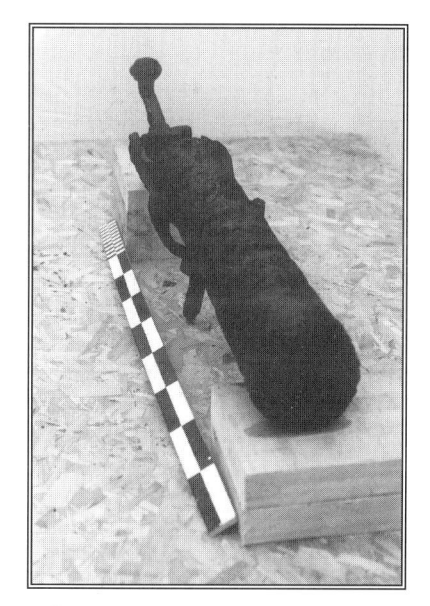

Swivel gun from one of Mad Joanna's ships". Picture: Tony Aylmer.

Neville Oldham with a Swedish finbanker cannon from the Erme mouth, which is about to be lowered into a conservation tank. Picture: Bernard Eaton.

Each dive confused them more. A small cast bronze figure of a woman was found and given a provisional dating of AD500 and a possible origin as Spain. A bronze pestle could be of any age. Bar-shot on the seabed near the cannons seemed to match with those of the 17th century. Close by lay a set of crowbars, probably used to lever the gun carriages around on the deck.

It was soon clear that the mouth of the Erme was home to more than a dozen wrecks. Research into old records found not only the two ships of Philip and Joanna, but "a significant wreck" noted for January 13, 1632; a French ship on February 20, 1637; a Genoese ship on February 21, 1668; a Dutch ship on November 29, 1691; another French ship on February 1, 1695; one unidentified in December, 1698; the *Rochester*, formerly called *Hope* in 1700; *HMS Pigmy* on December 15, 1793; the *St. Juan Baptista* on November 24, 1795; the *Caroline* in December, 1851; and the *Commerce de Paris*, laden with cotton, in 1869.

The site of the wrecks has been protected by being designated under the Protection of Wrecks Act by the Department of the Environment. This protection order bans any diving or other disturbance of the wrecks.

Foot Note: The reason that the mouth of the Erme is such a graveyard of shipping is simply that from seaward at high tide it looks like the perfect shelter, almost a harbour, certainly a safe anchorage. But in reality, it is a deadly trap. Across the entrance and out of sight except at all but low water is the reef called Mary's Rocks, just waiting to rip the bottom out of any ship which runs in.

You should keep your eyes open when on either Mothecombe or Wonwell beaches as it was here that broken pieces of ancient pottery of Mediterranean origin, probably from one of the wrecks, were picked up in 1962.

There is no ferry here and to get across from Mothecombe to Wonwell means wading. The river can usually be waded one hour each side of low water. Do not attempt to cross if there is floodwater coming down river or if on-shore winds are driving heavy seas into the estuary.

The dark shapes of Mary's Rocks can be seen through the water from the cliff as you climb up towards Beacon Point. They are partially exposed at low, but at high water can be covered by as much as six feet of water.

Back from the Bronze Age. Divers Jim Tyson and Ron Howell hand the first of the tin ingots to project leader Neville Oldham. (See Wreck No. 2, next page). Picture: Tony Aylmer.

2. BRONZE AGE TIN TRADER.
Erme Mouth. 1000BC.

HAVING found remains of such an assortment of ships in the mouth of the Erme, it is not surprising that the divers spread their search wider and wider around the original finds. It was on one such sweep that their underwater metal detector went mad.

And kept going mad 42 times in all! The divers had found the cargo of an ancient tin trader - 42 odd-shaped ingots of almost pure tin. This was clearly the 14th wreck to be credited to that reef lying across the mouth of the Erme - a wreck which is one of the oldest ever discovered in Britain.

The wood of that wreck had long gone. All that seemed to be left was her cargo of ingots. They were of various sizes. The largest was 41cms long by 21cms wide with a depth of 6.5cms and weighed nearly 13 kilos. The smallest was a midget of 7.8cms, which weighed less than a quarter of a kilo. But they all had one thing in common. They had all been formed by scooping out a mould in the earth and pouring the molten metal into it. This resulted in one side of each ingot being flat and smooth and the other bumpy with the odd stone embedded in it. It is one of the earliest known methods of making ingots and dates right back to the Bronze Age.

It was a sensational find. It became even more sensational when the ingots under analysis and scientific dating were indeed from the Bronze Age. It was no wonder that archaeologists were soon drooling over the Erme ingots calling them "the most important collection of tin ingots ever discovered in Britain".

The site was immediately designated and protected by means of the Protection of Wrecks Act. This, together with the protection of the ships of Joanna of Castille (see Wreck No.1), means that most of the mouth of the Erme Estuary is now recognised as the site of wrecks of historic importance.

The discovery may well lead to the rewriting of the history of Britain, certainly of Devon. It certainly means rewriting the history of the tin trade with Britain and the way they brought the tin down from mines on Dartmoor. For the discovery spotlighted the mystery which has always surrounded Burgh Island, a short distance along the coast to the east and within easy sight of the mouth of the Erme (see Wreck No.6).

3. PERSIER
Challaborough, 1945

ALTHOUGH Oberleutnant Werner Riecken and his crew of 34 in *UB-1017* torpedoed the *Persier* on February 11, 1945, he didn't see her sink – and nor did anyone else. No one knew where she was until a rod-and-line fisherman kept losing his tackle and told Plymouth divers about it. Those divers found her in May, 1969.

The story of the last voyage of the *Persier* begins on February 8, 1945. She left Cardiff on a mercy mission – to take food to the liberated, but starving people of Belgium. There were 63 people on board the ship when she sailed, some of them survivors of the *Leopoldville*, which, torpedoed, sank off Cherbourg on Christmas night, 1944. These survivors had asked to be repatriated and as the *Persier* was the first ship to head for a Belgian port, they were put aboard. For this voyage the 5382-ton Belgian steamer, which had originally been called the *War Buffalo* when she was launched at Newcastle in 1918, was to be part of Convoy No. BTC 65. The convoy commander, Commodore Edmund Wood and his staff of three signallers were based aboard her.

On February 11, the convoy was between the Eddystone and the shore when Commodore Wood received a message from one of the small escort ships that one of the convoy had reported seeing a periscope. Not long afterwards a column of water shot skywards on the port side of the convoy. Older hands guessed that it was the premature explosion of a German torpedo. They were right. Within seconds another torpedo hissed past the stern of the *Persier* from port to starboard and disappeared. On the bridge

The 5382-ton Persier was torpedoed while taking food to liberated Belgium.

Captain Mathieu, First Officer Lardinoy and Commodore Wood braced themselves. They knew what was coming and at 5.25pm precisely, it did.

The torpedo struck the port side opposite No.2 hold and just forward of the bridge. The explosion flung Lardinoy to the deck and broke his nose. On board *UB-1017* the crew believed they had hit two ships – the premature explosion of the earlier torpedo, they thought, was another hit. Riecken later reported two ships sunk.

On board *Persier*, as the sea poured into the damaged hold, the boxes of powdered egg, tins of baby food and meat, broke loose and five tons of woollen blankets soaked up the sea. The ship started to list to port. Abandon ship drill took only six minutes, but it went terribly wrong. Lifeboat No.1, with Commodore Wood and ten others, was launched correctly, but the enormous seas unhooked the bow and left it suspended by the stern, spilling everyone into the water. Lifeboat No.3 was drawn into the ship's still-spinning propellor and was chopped to pieces. Lifeboat No.1 was then righted, but as three men slid down the falls to her, one, a stoker, caught his foot and was left hanging, smashed against the side of the ship by every wave. The two other men fared little better reaching the boat safely, but it was then also drawn into the propeller.

The ship was now about four miles from the Eddystone in winds of Force 7. The seas were colossal. Rafts were launched and men managed to cling to them. The *Persier* had stopped moving, with her propellor still. But she was obviously not long for the surface. Her stern was right out of the water. Still aboard were her captain, Lardinoy, and five others. It was then that Lardinoy put forward a desperate idea. He would swim to a nearby small cargo ship, the *Birker Force* and ask the captain to come alongside and rescue them. To get him away from the ship, he asked the other men to throw him as far out as they could. That is what they did. Lardinoy, despite being thumped by nearby depth-charging, managed to swim to a lifeboat which had been launched from the *Birker Force* and gasped out his message. As the ship moved in on the *Persier*, the men on board flung an old unseaworthy raft in to the sea and jumped for it. They were all picked up. In all, 44 were saved out of the *Persier*'s complement of 63. *Persier* was last seen drifting into the night, stern high, bow down. Tugs sent out from Plymouth searched in vain.

She sank in the dark and no one saw her going. And no one would know where she was today if Colin Hopkins, chairman then of Plymouth Sound branch of the British Sub-Aqua Club, after being told by a sea-angling friend of a place he was always losing tackle, dived the site and found the wreck of a large armed merchantman with a 4.7in gun on her stern and two sets of Oerlikon guns, one on the stern and one on the bridge. She had a bronze propellor. Plymouth Sound BSAC confirmed her name when they recovered her bell – still clearly marked War Buffalo. They bought the *Persier* for £300 and 12 members of the branch put up the money. They got their money back when they raised and sold her bronze propellor.

Foot Note: The *Persier* today is right off Challaborough and a good way towards the mouth of the Erme. Her bows point to the south-west. When she sank, though nobody actually saw the sinking, her cargo was soon spread along the beaches in the neighbourhood, particularly those of Bantham and Thurlestone. Goods that were strictly rationed lay all along the tideline. People came from miles around for the tons of "Sunlight" soap, tins of sausages, tins of pork, tins of biscuits and 20lb packages of powdered egg. The Customs men arrived too, but just as in days of long ago, a great deal of the goods went into hiding in the cottages and barns roundabout. Some of the soap is still hidden in Thurlestone and supplies at least one villager's needs to this day!

4. DUTCH WARSHIP.
Burgh Island, 1670

IN 60 feet of water off Challaborough, divers have, on four completely separate occasions, found beautiful little bronze cannon, which must mean an old wreck in the area.

Roy Wardle, a keen South London diver, found one – lying on the sand with the muzzle sticking out from under a flat rock. The bright green told him that it was bronze. When cleaned it was just under two feet long, with little lifting dolphins. Unfortunately the crest on the first reinforce was too badly worn to be made out. The touchhole had been rebushed at some time and the latch-cover was missing. But the cascabel is a great work of art, completely circled by beautiful little bronze leaves clustering round the acorn of the handle. The bore is one-and-a- half inches in diameter.

Roy Wardle found his cannon in 1974. About the same time and in exactly the same area, a Guildford diver found its twin sister! And then in 1977, Geoffrey Moles, a founder member of St Albans BS-AC, found yet another bronze gun - a bigger sister to the twins - 30 inches long, weighing 60lbs, and bearing

Roy Wardle with one of the little bronze guns which he found off Burgh Island.

Diver Geoff Moles found this bigger bronze cannon nearby.

the date 1670. This one had the right-hand dolphin (looking from the cascabel forward) missing and so was the latch-cover over the touchhole. Geoff Moles says that he was diving in gin-clear water over slate gullies in 20m. He saw the "bright green" gun from 25 feet away. It was out in the open on top of one of the slate ridges. He clipped the caribineer of his buoy line to the remaining dolphin and searched around for anything else. He found nothing. On examination the cannon was found to be unloaded. The bore was once again one-and-a-half inches.

It seems almost unbelievable, but another St.Albans diver found this bigger gun's twin, even down to the same missing dolphin, not far from the site of the first, but lying on sand in the bottom of one of the slate gullies.

The four guns have been identified with the help of the coat of arms on the two larger ones as "probably Dutch",and that, and the date on them, rules out the two ships of Philip of Castile which were lost in the mouth of the Erme in January 1506.

There was a Dutch ship lost in the area on November 29,1691. We don't know her name only that five or six of her crew were lost and that she was registered in Holland and on passage from the Canary Islands.

These dividers and bronze rings inset with red glass "stones" were found below the tide line on Bigbury beach with a metal detector.

There was another Dutch ship, the *Annatiere Helena*, wrecked and looted at Thurlestone in 1738. And there was a Hamburg-bound Dutch "galliott" laden with wine, brandy, coffee and indigo on January 10/11,1753, stranded at Thurlestone, but as much of her cargo was saved, it is unlikely they would have left the guns (see Wreck No.12).

The belief that the wreck took place close to or on Burgh Island was strengthened when a man using a metal detector on the sand at Bigbury-on-Sea found a pair of bronze dividers bearing the same fleur-de-lis marking as appeared on the cannon. Some large bronze rings inset with coloured stones found nearby, suggest that the ship's fittings were much decorated. That together with the bronze cannon suggest that this was an important ship and it is strange that the wreck appears not to have been reported.

5. DAGGER.
Bantham Harbour. 1736

THERE is a chance that the bronze guns found around Burgh Island came from a much later ship. And not necessarily a Dutch one either. Such expensive decorated guns would last at least a century at sea, moving from ship to ship, either captured or sold. One candidate for the guns in that case could be the *Dagger*, lost at Bantham in 1736.

We know she was carrying small guns because of an Admiralty Court held at Hope Cove on April 21, 1737 where people were summoned for not taking goods from the sea to the Earl of Devon's steward. Part of the records of that court reads: **"We present George Hamblin of Orford Jefford for taking up of a graper about fifty weight at the place the Dagger was cast away at Bantham harbour, 1736 . . . We present John Piles of Kingsbridge for taking up a small gun where the Dagger was lost . . ."**

The description of the *Dagger* being lost at "Bantham harbour", which seems to have meant the area both inside and outside the river mouth, is very vague. However, local divers have recently explored the reef of which Murray's Rock shows at Low and is marked with a beacon. This reef runs to the south-east from the tip of Burgh Island's south-east tip and is a hazard to boats intent on entering the Avon at Bantham. They found a large ancient anchor near the end of the reef furthest from the island. More diving is required for there may well be more bronze guns in the sea around Burgh Island and divers there are now alert for any glimpse of that bright green which bronze and brass go when underwater for any length of time.

Foot Note: The area around Bigbury is well known for the number of blackthorn or sloe bushes in the hedges. And for the amount of sloe gin the locals make from them! It is interesting to note that the name "Murray's Rock", a possible cause of the loss of the *Dagger,* may be a corruption of the old English word "merris" for wild cherries or sloes. You see, Murray's Rock was called the Merries in 1884, and in 1765 it was named as the Merris Rock. So was there a wild cherry tree on that rock long ago - or blackthorns laden with sloes?

6. VILLA NOVA
Burgh Island, 1879.

BURGH Island was known in olden times as "Burrow Island" or "Burrough Island" or "Burr Island" and those are the ways you will see it spelt on old maps and in many old wreck reports . . . "Hit Burrough Island" . . . "Struck edge of Burrow Island". It was quite common for sailing ship masters in poor weather to mistake Burgh Island for Looe Island, much further to the west, and a wreck often resulted. A classic case of this error, was the sinking of HMS *Ramillies*. (See Wreck No.21).

It was left, however, to Captain Walter Little of the *Villa Nova*, a brigantine in ballast from St Malo to Cardiff, to make the biggest error of all about the lie of the land in these parts. On December 27,1879, he thought Bolt Tail was Lands End and in attempting to round it went ashore on Burgh Island itself. The crew all saved themselves in their own boat and landed near Thurlestone.

Tin ingots from the Erme, showing their bottom sides with stones from the earth moulds embedded in them. The smallest and largest are shown. (See Wreck No. 2).

Foot Note: At low tide a causeway of firm sand leads from the shore at Bigbury to the island and you can walk across for a drink at the Pilchard Inn there. Beware leaving the return too late. The tide sweeps through at an amazing rate.

A tractor-wheeled passenger wagon, with the passenger-compartment perched high out of reach of the sea, makes crossings every half-hour when the tide is up in all but really bad weather. But the lifeboat did once have to rescue the passengers when even the tractor became stuck. The sand is firm – until the tide starts to soften it. Under the causeway is said to be at least one Army truck which left it too late!

Burgh Island is owned by Tony and Beatrice Porter, who have restored the 1920-style hotel and its restaurant, for which it is essential to book , especially during the summer season. It is said that the hotel was a get-away for Noel Coward and that Agatha Christie wrote "The Ten Little Niggers" there. The Beatles have stayed there and many a film and tv programme has featured the island.

But new discoveries show that the island may have had a very much bigger claim to fame in the very distant past. It now seems possible that this was the fabled island of Ictis, the Bronze Age centre for Britain's tin trade with Mediterranean and European countries.

The tin ingots recovered from the mouth of the River Erme by divers in 1993 (see Wreck No.2) have altered our knowledge of the marine history of Devon. We knew that early tin mining took place on Dartmoor, but recently archaeologists made a discovery of ancient tin slag which suggests that tin was mined near Princetown in prehistoric days. Those ancient miners would have made their ingots just as those from the Erme were made - pouring the molten metal into a scrape in the ground. And now it is tempting to think that those Dartmoor miners sent their tin down to the coast via the River Avon to Burgh Island to sell to foreign traders waiting there.

Until the Erme discovery, it was generally believed that the ancient tin trade with Britain was carried out solely from Cornwall. Archaeologists reading Diodorus Siculus, the first century BC Greek historian, noted that he wrote in about 10BC that the tin traders sailed to an island called Ictis, just off the main coastline of Britain, to buy the ingots from the natives and then took them back to Gaul where they were loaded on to horses for another 30-day journey to the Mediterraen. Ictis, wrote Diodorus, is left dry at low tide and then has a causeway of sand leading out to it from the shore along which the tin could be brought in wagons.

Until the Erme discovery, Ictis was believed to be St.Michael's Mount, near Penzance, Cornwall. But now when you see Burgh Island linked at low tide by that causeway of hard sand to the shore at Bigbury, you must think differently.

The Erme ingot finds explain so much. Explain the big stone anchors found at the mouth of the Avon (and used for a rockery in one local garden!). Explains the ancient settlement or trading centre across from Burgh Island on Bantham Ham's sand dunes, which when uncovered by storm waves showed pottery and implements dating back to the Bronze and Iron Ages. Explains too why there is another Bronze Age shipwreck only a few miles away along the coast at Moor Sand (see Wreck No.44).

The Aircraft Graveyard: A mile out to sea from the westerly tip of Burgh Island, divers have discovered the wings and bodies of World War aircraft such as the Catalina flying boat. There are no engines in the wreckage and no record of such aircraft being dumped there.

The top of Burgh Island was one of the lookout sites for spotting the huge pilchard shoals which brought prosperity to Bantham, Bigbury and Challaborough in the years between 1750 and 1866. When you cross the Avon by ferry (check times with the Bantham Harbourmaster) to the Bantham side, you will walk up from the ferry past a building named the Pilchard Cellars and dated 1779. A little farther up where the little road makes a sharp right turn is a stone building which looks like a lime kiln, but is in fact all that remains of the place many of the fish were cured. The pilchard fishermen of Bantham, Bigbury and Challaborough could catch a total of 12 million pilchards in a day! And continued to do so until the massive shoals of fish stopped coming around 1870. The catch cured at Bantham was exported to France, Italy and Spain. The oil pressed out of them was used in lamps all around the district. Smelly but effective. Along a public footpath from Bantham towards Aveton Gifford at Aunemouth are the ruins of the pilchard fishermen's own village at the river's edge.

SECTION TWO –
Bantham to Beacon Point.

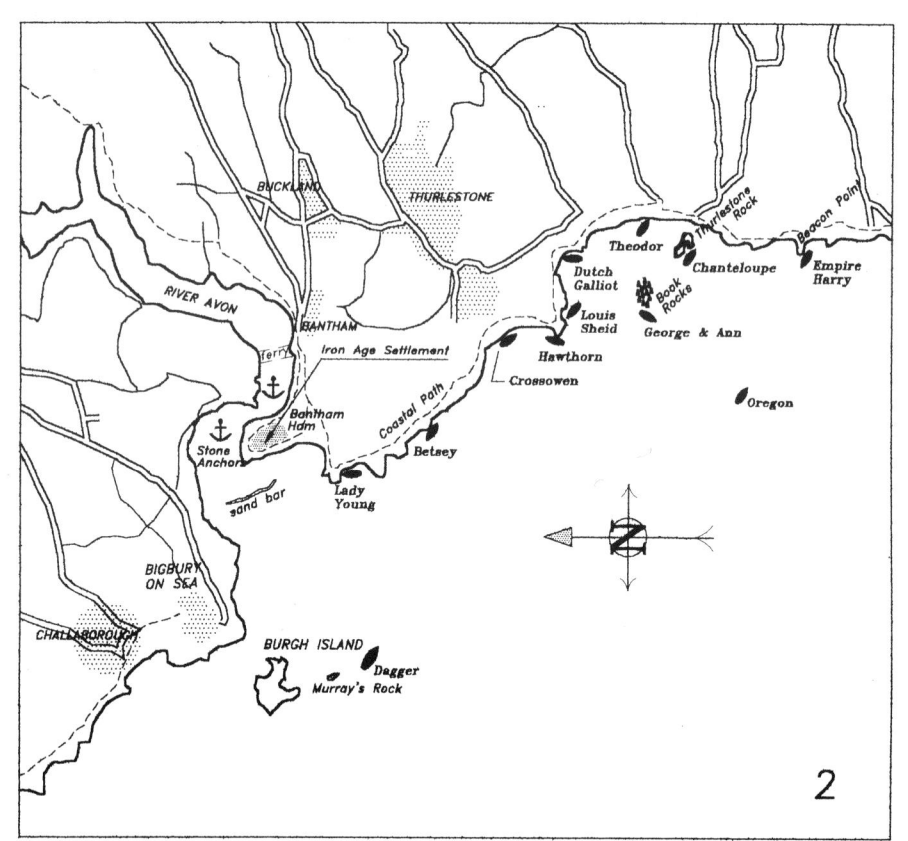

7. LADY YOUNG
Long Stone, Bantham, 1880.

THE gale came out of the south-south-west and drove all before it. Huge waves shot up Bolt Tail in white fireworks of spray. As night came on and the tide rose, the sea scooped sand in great bites out of the dunes of Bantham Ham. Not far out to sea in Bigbury Bay, a barque was losing the battle to stay offshore. It was October 27, 1880.

That sailing ship was the *Lady Young*, of 589 tons, registered at Liverpool, and bound from Hamburg to Cardiff. Captain John Watkins and his 13-man crew were in trouble, but they were not the only ones. All round the southern half of Britain ships were in distress from that same gale, which was officially reported as "very heavy". That means that the winds were of near-hurricane force.

Captain Watkins was trying to reach the shelter of Plymouth Sound, but the gale blew away some of his sails and damaged his masts. He found himself inside Bolt Tail

The Lady Young was in ballast when she was wrecked in October, 1880. Burgh Island is in the background.

and fired distress signals. They were answered by Hope Cove Coastguard, but the *Lady Young* was finally blown ashore further to the west between West Down Point, Bantham and the Long Stone, a tall pillar of rock, which still juts up from the sea just off today's coastal path.

By 1a.m., the 144ft-long ship was firmly on the rocks, upright, but with the sea beginning to smash her bottom out in the lift and fall of the waves. She was well in towards the shore because she had been in ballast and riding high.

At this moment, John Watkins ordered more distress signals to be lit. This time it was to be Challaborough Coastguards who responded.

In 1880, Challaborough was an important coastguard station with five men stationed there under the command of Captain Ommaney. But as they were the other side of the River Avon, it was not until 4 a.m. that they were able to get their rocket apparatus to the cliff top and fire a rocket line down to the ship some 50 feet below them. But even with the help of Mr.John Hoskins and Mr.Philip Mann and others from the cottages at Bantham, it wasn't until nearly 6 a.m. that they had the bosun's chair rigged and were ready to bring the first men ashore.

What happened then is not entirely clear. Most of the crew were foreigners; Captain Watkins and the steward, John Nabsley of Reigate, Surrey, were said to be the only Englishmen aboard. All but the steward were brought ashore safely. One version of what happened says that Nabsley put all his clothing and belongings into the chair or basket of the rocket rescue apparatus when it was his turn, and then sat on top. Then, as he was being hauled up to the cliff top, he slipped off and fell to his death on the rocks below and his body was washed out to sea.

Another version says that the steward was brought safely to shore and was then allowed to go back to get his belongings and that he fell on this return trip.

This Illustrated London News drawing of the time does show the bosun's chair containing some packages, but their written report makes no mention of any return trip. It says: **"One of the crew of the barque that got aground at Bantham, while he was being passed along the rope stretched across from the stranded vessel to the summit of the cliff, where the Coastguard men were hauling him in, lost his hold of the rope and fell headlong into the sea where he instantly perished"**.

The *Lady Young*, which had been built of the finest wood in Quebec, Canada, in 1870, was a total wreck and was broken up by the sea in the days following the wreck. Wood and other items from the wreck were sold by auction. Captain John Watkins was not blamed for her loss and went on to command two bigger sailing ships, the *Clwyd* and the *County of Merioneth*.

Foot Note: West Down Point is the first headland that the path climbs up from the eastern end of Bantham beach, which now attracts surfers from near and far. The Long Stone is obvious.

The highest point on the golf course lies almost directly inland along the public footpath at the western edge of the course. That high point was once known as Beacon Field - it was where the beacon was lit to warn of the coming of the Spanish Armada. However, the field you cross by the Long Stone cliff edge has an even earlier historical significance. It is known to this day as "Ireland". It is likely to be where three sons of King Harold, of arrow-in-the-eye and 1066 defeat, camped when they returned to Britain in 1069 with Irish and Danish pirates and extracted some revenge for the death of their father by burning and looting some of the 107 manors and villages given by William the

Conqueror to Juhel, his greatest military commander, as a reward for the Norman conquest of the South-West (See Wreck No.10).

If you want to see some of the wood of the *Lady Young* you should walk into Bantham itself and just opposite and to the right of the Sloop Inn, you will see a building which was once quarters for coastguards. A lot of the wood used in building that house came from the *Lady Young*.

Builder of those coastguard quarters was the Reverend Peregrine Ilbert, Rector of Thurlestone from 1839 to 1895. Mr.Ilbert was what we should call today a dedicated D.I.Y. man. He loved building and carpentry. In fact he built a complete new rectory in Thurlestone (today called the Old Rectory)And he was always excited and pleased when a ship came ashore - though only because it gave him plenty of wood! He was to the forefront of the auction of the pieces of the *Lady Young*, buying bunks and other wood for his Bantham building.

He also bid successfully for the carved figurehead of the ship which he built into the hallway of a cottage he was converting in nearby West Buckland called "Peep o' Day". It is there to this day.

The figurehead of the Lady Young was cut out of a wooden disc amid the ornate carving of her bow.

8. BETSEY
Loam Castle, Thurlestone. 1816

PRISONERS taken by British troops from Napoleon's armies became a damned nuisance. The prisons and prison hulks in Plymouth Harbour were soon full to overflowing. Which is why Prince's Town and Dartmoor Prison came to be built.

Both town and prison are the result of the enthusiasm of Sir Thomas Tyrwhitt, a close friend and secretary of the Prince Regent after whom the little town on the moor is named.

Today we write it as one word, Princetown , but then there was nothing to be seen of the little town which today surrounds the prison 1400 feet up on Dartmoor. However, Sir Thomas was convinced that the moor could be made productive and profitable and he started growing flax and quarrying granite. He built a village at Prince's Town to house his workers. He added an inn, called the Plume of Feathers after his royal patron, but still couldn't get the workmen he needed to live there and brave the bitter winds, cold mists, rain and snowfalls of winter.

In 1805, Sir Thomas had a brainwave. If a prison were built at Prince's Town to take the ever-increasing number of French prisoners-of-war, then they could work in his fields and quarries.

The prison was completed in 1809 at a cost of £127,000. It covered 30 acres surrounded by double walls and contained a hospital, a covered exercise yard and five buildings to house the prisoners, Despite the fact that these buildings were only 300 feet long and 50 feet wide, the prison soon held 10,000 prisoners.

As soon as Waterloo was won and the war ended, we wanted to get rid of them. The cost of feeding 10,000 prisoners was no small sum. So they were sent home as soon as possible. They went in batches. Not all the way, of course, just to the nearest French port.

There were 65 men in the batch who were taken down in carts from the prison to the small ship called *Betsey* in

Plymouth docks on Saturday, January 6th, 1816. Snow lay on the Moor as they rumbled out of the big main gate with its carved motto "Parcere subjectis" (Spare the conquered). The men in the carts were all captains and lieutenants of highly-respected French cavalry regiments - the 20th Regiment of Cuirassiers, the 4th Regiment of Chasseurs, and the Young Guard of the Horse Chasseurs.

It was almost as cold in Plymouth dockyard as up on the Moor, but the Captain and crew of the *Betsey* made the men as comfortable as they could. Even so that Saturday night must have been an ordeal in such a small ship. The *Betsey* was described in The Times of Monday, January 15, 1816 as a "cartel". A "cartel" is not a type of ship, but a description of a ship being used for exchanging prisoners. That presumably meant that at Roscoff in France, a similar number of British prisoners were waiting for the *Betsey* to bring them home.

On Sunday at dawn they sailed, but the ship wasn't far out of Plymouth Sound when the weather began to worsen. All Sunday they fought the wind, but it was obvious that the ship was losing the battle. During that night, the Captain ordered all sails down and hove-to to try and ride out the enormous seas. But when Monday dawned, he saw he was trapped in Bigbury Bay. Though he tried every sailing trick he knew, the *Betsey* was driven on shore near Thurlestone and close to the distinctive point known as Loam Castle, just to the east of the cove called Broad Sands.

Great seas rolled the *Betsey* over, spilling the men into the surf and on to the razor-sharp granite and slate reefs which run out from the shore. Twenty-eight Frenchmen died there and many of the survivors were badly hurt by the cutting edge of those rocks.

Foot Note: The bodies of 19 French prisoners are recorded in the parish church register as being buried in Thurlestone churchyard, though if you take one of the footpaths across the golf course from the coast path to the 11th century All Saints Church at the foot of the village, you will look in vain for any stone marking the grave or graves. You will see though some of the slate gravestones of the time, which have fallen and are now propped along the rear wall of the graveyard. From these stones you will see how badly slate weathers and how indecipherable are some of the stones of that period. The 11th century church, however, is well worth a visit, the porch dates back to Henry VIII's reign and its roof was the hiding place for kegs of brandy on many a smuggling run (see Wreck No.9).

9. CROSSOWEN
Yarmouth Sands 1908

THURLESTONE'S *Mary Celeste*. That is what the brigantine *Crossowen* appeared to be when found with all sails set, but no one aboard, at Yarmouth Sands, Thurlestone, in the dawn of Friday, May 7, 1908. Like the *Mary Celeste*, what happened to make the *Crossowen*'s crew abandon her remains a mystery to this day.

The question of what happened to her crew was soon answered. Over the next few days the bodies of six crewmen and a boy, presumed to have also been aboard, were washed ashore in, and around, the mouth of the River Avon at Bantham. An upturned boat was found on nearby Bantham Sands.

What happened to the ship and why her crew abandoned her is more difficult to discover. The previous night the coast had been wrapped in a thick fog, despite a strong south-westerly wind The sound of guns were heard at 9.30 p.m. on that foggy Thursday evening in the village of Thurlestone, but the villagers heard guns so often from Naval practices that they had no thought that the sounds were signals of distress. As it turned out later, if the gunfire was a signal of distress, it certainly did not come from the *Crossowen*, which did not carry a signal gun.

The ship was first seen by two Thurlestone men on their way to work in a small local quarry. They told coastguards at Bantham and the Hope Cove lifeboat was launched. So was the coastguards' galley, an open boat with places for six oarsmen. However, neither could get close to the wreck because of the big seas. Nor, because of the thick fog around her, could the ship's name be made out until nearly 9 a.m. By then the first body had been found at Bantham.

Wreck of Crossowen, Yarmer Sands, Thurleston. May

The sight of the ship with all sails set attracted a huge crowd of people from all over the district. At 5.30 p.m. the tide was thought low enough to make an attempt to board the ship, and a young naval seaman home on leave called Ingram, of nearby South Milton, waded and swam out to her carrying a rope from a team of coastguards standing on rocks about 20 yards from the ship's stern, but he was knocked over by the breakers and after several more tries, Lieutenant Helby of the coastguards ordered him to stop. It was not until much later on the next tide that the seas had calmed enough to let anyone board. There was no one aboard and all the signs that the crew had left in a hurry.

Local experts thought that the crew had abandoned the vessel after she had struck the rocks at the tip of Burgh Island. In the fog, they had rowed towards the sound of breakers thinking that they would find a beach to land on, but instead had run into the dangerous breakers of Bantham Bar, a big sandbank near the mouth of the Avon, and the boat had overturned. The experts thought too that the *Crossowen* was stuck on the rocks of Burgh Island at the time when the crew left her, but the rising tide had floated her free and she sailed on to beach at the western end of Yarmouth Sands.

The inquest was opened at the Village Inn, Bantham. Mr.Henry Clark of Bantham, whose wife was laying out the bodies - each had a cross of flowers and a bunch of roses on the breast - was chosen foreman of the jury. The owner of the *Crossowen*, William Charles Phillips of Mount Charles, St.Austell, Cornwall, told the jury that he owned the ship with his brother. Her captain was George Roger Hitchens, a widower of Charlestown, Cornwall. The ship had sailed from Fowey at four in the afternoon on Thursday for Leith with a cargo of china clay.

Captain Hitchens' body, when picked up in the River Avon, had been found to have the ship's papers in his pocket together with a watch which had stopped at 23 minutes to six. The coroner then adjourned the inquest until Tuesday to enable more of the bodies to be identified. The resumed inquest was held at Thurlestone. The coroner asked the jury to walk over to Bantham to view the bodies and when they returned, heard more evidence. James Start, the Chief Officer of the coastguard at Hope Cove said that he launched his own boat and sailed down to the wreck. He found the surf too great to get close and though he thought he saw someone aboard it turned out to be the top of a ventilation funnel sticking up above the companion hatch. The *Crossowen* must have gone ashore at high tide to get where she was. That was about 11 o'clock. If it had been earlier she would have torn her bottom out on the rocks.

Coroner: You think she was abandoned before she got to the beach?" Mr.Start: "Yes, anyone who has been at sea could not conceive of a captain of his age abandoning his

The Crossowen stayed on the rocks until big seas broke her up.

vessel in a place like that. There would have been no danger to the crew with the sea which was running. The vessel has stuck and she will stick there for another six months unless we get heavy seas".

Coroner:"Why do you think she was abandoned?"

Mr.Start: "My theory is that she struck something on the outer edge of Burgh Island and was making water. Perhaps the crew got panic-stricken and lowered the boat and told the captain that if he liked to remain he could...of course that is only a theory I can never conceive any crew leaving a vessel with the sea running that night. It was not a big sea".

The coroner summing up said that it was inexplicable why the *Crossowen* did not use her foghorn. It was in the captain's cabin and had not been used at all. The coastguard had put forward a theory. It might be an explanation, but they would never know. The jury returned a verdict of accidentally drowned.

The bodies were buried in Thurlestone churchyard. The 242-ton *Crossowen*, which had been built in Grangemouth, near Falkirk, in 1878, and registered in Glasgow, was found to be badly holed and became a total wreck during a storm a fortnight later.

Foot Note: The pick-up point on the western bank of the passenger ferry, which operates at limited times, across the

River Avon at Bantham, is almost exactly where Henry Bevell of Bantham recovered the body of the *Crossowen*'s captain and found the ship's papers in his pocket.

Do not attempt to wade the Avon at any time. There are deep holes in many places.

The village inn in Bantham where part of the inquest was held is the Sloop Inn, known today for its fine food restaurant and excellent "pub grub"(worth a diversion from the path!)

You won't find many people who call the sands where the brigantine came ashore "Yarmouth". "Yarmer" is the local name for this popular bathing beach. There is a pathway across the golf course to the village of Thurlestone.

Old documents show that Yarmer was a favourite landing place for smugglers. The kegs were put ashore there and then carried across the Warren, now the golf course, to Thurlestone Church where they were hidden behind the battlements on the roof of the church porch. While as many as 50 small barrels of brandy were stowed there, the churchwarden would conveniently lose the key to the church tower - for the top of the tower was the only place from which the cache could be seen!

10. HAWTHORN
Warren Point, Thurlestone, 1881.

THE *Hawthorn* wreck is another tale of a ship ashore with no one aboard. It is not clear why her crew abandoned her. The 296-ton barque *Hawthorn* came ashore stern first on Warren Point on Tuesday morning March 8,1881. Her cargo of sugar in bags was still aboard, but all her ten crew and her captain, Charles Mead, had left her. This was surprising because she had ridden out the gale which had driven the *Volere* ashore on the Bolt a day or two earlier (Wreck No. 30) and though her head or forward sails were gone, all her square sails were still set.

A man from South Milton had seen her out in the Channel in the storm on the Monday. As he watched, a French steamer, the *Albert*, went alongside and then pulled away from her. On the Tuesday when she was spotted near the Delvers, which are the rocks running out from Warren Point, a Hope coastguard called out the Hope lifeboat, but before they could reach her she had struck and started breaking up in the big swell from the storm. Her logbook was picked up from the sea and had no entry in it after a normal entry on the previous Sunday. From the logbook it could be seen that the Hawthorn had left Pernambuco (now Recife) in Brazil on January 20 and had intended to call at Falmouth for orders. The *Albert* landed the crew at Dunkirk where they told the authorities that their ship had started sinking.

Divers recently found the *Hawthorn*'s anchors and some of her square portholes in the sea just off Warren Point.

Foot Note: The footpath round the edge of Thurlestone Golf Course goes right by Warren Point, whose little cove has the intriguing name of Ireland Sands. This may be one of the landing places of Irish pirates led by the sons of King Harold in 1069 when they were seeking revenge for that arrow in their father's eye three years earlier. They looted and burned their way along the coast to Salcombe before sailing away (see Wreck No.7).

11. LOUIS SHEID
Leas Foot, Thurlestone, 1939

NO torpedo touched her. Nor did the white wake of one come near her. But there is no doubt that the blame for this ship running ashore on December 8, 1939, at Leas Foot, close to Thurlestone Golf Club, must go to Korvettenkapitan Gunther Prien, the German war hero, whom Hitler had personally decorated with the Knights Cross with Oak Leaves for sinking the Royal Oak in Scapa Flow less than two months earlier. For it was fear of Prien in *U-47* that sent the *Louis Sheid* much too close into the shelter of the coast.

The *Louis Sheid* was a big ship – 6057 tons, 418ft with a beam of 55ft. She was built in 1920 by Nord Werft of

The Louis Sheid after the rescue of her crew and the survivors of another ship by both lifeboat and rocket line at Thurlestone in 1939.

Wesermunde as the *Ultor* for the Rickmers Line before being renamed *Kendal Castle* for the James Chambers Lancashire Shipping Company of Liverpool, and then finally named again *Louis Sheid* when bought by the Belgian National Shipping Line.

In the early morning of December 7, 1939, there was no doubt about the her allegiance. Homeward bound from Buenos Aires for Antwerp with a main cargo of grain, plus 600 tons of hides and 12 tons of leaf tobacco and honey, and a crew of 46, the word "BELGIE" was painted in huge white letters on her sides, together with a big Belgian flag, for if Britain was at war with Germany, Belgium was not.

Nor, for that matter, was Holland, but neutrality did not save the 8159 ton cargo-liner *Tajandoen*, bound from Amsterdam for Batavia with 14 passengers and a general cargo of cement, iron, glassware, mild steel sheet, aniline

The end result of south-westerly gales. The Louis Sheid in two in 1940

and pharmaceutical products. Gunther Prien started to line up on her at 5.24am and hit her with one torpedo at 5.30. The great explosion was heard clearly on board the *Louis Sheid*.

The Dutch ship began to sink almost at once. The torpedo's explosion had split her fuel tanks and fuel covered the sea around her. Six crew didn't reach the lifeboats when they were lowered and probably died in the torpedo hit. The 62 who did make the boats had no sooner done so than the fuel oil around the ship ignited. The men rowed madly across the blazing sea and, scorched and singed, managed to reach the safety of the *Louis Sheid*.

Once the captain of the *Louis Sheid* had the *Tajandoen* survivors safely aboard, he feared that he might share the Dutch ship's fate. Prien and *U-47* were obviously no respecters of neutrality, so the *Louis Sheid* made off at full speed for the nearest land and shallow waters where the U-boat might not dare to go.

By nightfall the *Sheid* was running close in along the South Devon coast. Heavy rainfall blocked out the shape of the land and the wind was increasing into a full southerly gale. There were no friendly shore lights to guide her – blackout regulations made sure of that. Soon the ship was heading nearer and nearer in towards shore and finally, just missing the rocks they call the Delvers, reaching out from Warren Point, ran into the tiny bay of Leas Foot in front of the Thurlestone Golf Club. At the eastern end of that little shingle beach another small headland with a tiny reef at its foot was waiting. There the *Louis Sheid* struck, with a mighty crash, just as the tide was dropping.

The ship was within a few yards of the Links Hotel, now a block of flats called Links Court. She did not strand unnoticed. Jack Jarvis, the former cox'n of the old Hope Cove lifeboat, saw it happen and phoned the Salcombe lifeboat. The Salcombe boat has a hellish journey round the Bolt in enormous seas and finally found the ship two hours later.

It was only when they came alongside – rising and falling 20ft with the waves – and 40 men jumped into the boat, that Cox'n Eddie Distin found he was rescuing not one crew but two. All the first 40 men came from the *Tajandoen*.

The lifeboat made two trips, taking off all the Dutchmen first and landing them on Hope Cove, where local fisherman dared enormous waves to set up a ferry service between lifeboat and shore. When the Salcombe boat went back for the third time, the *Louis Sheid* had been moved by the wind and sea and the rising tide. She was now broadside under the cliffs and almost impossible to approach from the sea.

So the rocket apparatus was set up by the coastguards on the cliff overlooking her and the team soon had a line aboard. All the rest of the men came off safely that way. Eddie Distin was awarded the RNLI silver medal for the rescue and each of his crew, the Bronze. The *Louis Sheid*, despite many attempts to shift her, never moved again. The hides and tobacco were salvaged, but the grain was slowly washed out of her on to the nearby beaches. All further attempts at salvage were abandoned in 1940 after southwesterly gales broke her in two. In 1942 her bow collapsed and then they started cutting metal off her to be melted down and reused in the war effort. For one of these metal salvage operations, an aerial ropeway was set up the cliffs and was driven by a traction engine. After the war she was sold for £400 and more metal was brought ashore.

Foot Note: Cliff falls have closed the road which used to run across the front of the links Hotel, now the block of flats called Links Court, and the road has been re-established a little way inland. The very broken wreck of the *Louis Sheid* lies in 30 feet of water just off the shingle beach of Leas Foot bay and is much visited by divers. At full low her stempost and another piece of wreckage break the surface and you will often see divers in inflatable boats anchored over her three boilers, which are still sitting upright on the bottom.

It was here on Leas Foot in 1998 that a local resident walking along the beach in the morning after a night of great winds and huge waves, spotted a bright green "stone" left behind by the tide. Such a bright green is a dead giveaway for pieces of brass or copper left long in the sea. Moments later he was holding in his hands a Bronze Age spearhead nearly a foot long. So perfect was it that it was clear it had never been fitted to a shaft or flung in anger. It may well be evidence of a shipwreck nearby of some arms trader of 3,000 years ago (see Wrecks No.2, No. 6.and No.44).

12. DUTCH GALLIOT
Thurlestone Sands 1753

TEN thousand people gathered to plunder this small single-masted Dutch ship, which was driven ashore on Thurlestone Sands at the beginning of January, 1753 when homeward bound to Hamburg from the Greek island of Zante. She had a cargo of wine, brandy, coffee and herbs.

It was only because soldiers with fixed bayonets confronted the mob that the ship wasn't torn to pieces. Even that wouldn't have stopped the looting but one of the ringleaders "fell on one of the soldiers bayonnet" and was killed. This nasty "accident" cooled the situation remarkably quickly!

Such a huge gathering at a shipwreck may surprise you, but it was not uncommon as you will see when you read the section on the *Chantelope* (see Wreck No.14). In fact when a sailing ship was caught inshore with an onshore wind, people would gather from tens of miles around to watch and hope she would not get free. The ship's agony could take days and the crowds would move along the coast along the route of today's coastal path - as the ship moved back and forth tacking to try and get out to the open sea. It seems incredible that these crowds of on-lookers - you could hardly describe them as well-wishers - would get so big and that the news of a ship in trouble would spread so wide and so fast. In fact they grew in size dependent on the number of days the ship was trapped. The longer the actual wreck took to happen, the more people waited on the shore. Today it is easy to condemn them, but a "good wreck" could bring them more money than they could earn in a year and might make the difference between life and death in a hard winter. A single plank of wood might be worth more than a month's wages.

Daniel Defoe, of *Robinson Crusoe* fame, wrote during a visit to the West Country about "**the sands covered in people, they are charged with strange bloody and cruel dealings, even sometimes with one another, but especially with poor distressed seamen who seek for help for their lives and find the rocks themselves not more cruel and merciless than the people who range about them for their prey**".

Unfortunately, from the shipwrecked sailor's point of view, the laws about unclaimed wreck were almost an incitement to murder him as he staggered ashore.

Any wreck was worth a lot of money. And so the lords of the manors of the South Hams were delighted when they were awarded the right to unclaimed wreck on October 12, 1340, by Edward III. It was a right they guarded jealously and made sure that the laws about unclaimed wreck were known to all coastal dwellers on their land: The important sections of those laws were:

"**Whosoever finds any wrecked goods ought to carry it to the chief inhabitants of the town or place next to where it was found, and there to remain until a claim be made to it, either by any person saved alive belonging to the ship, or their wives, children, or executors, owner, merchant, or such has a good title to the land.**

"**And if no claim be made within a year and a day, then it must be delivered to the Admiral, or such hath the Royal privilege of the Royalty, paying reasonable for their trouble for salvage.**

"**If any man or living thing escape to shore alive, it is no wreck.**

"**If any one should have a lanthorne or make a light in order to subject them in danger of shipwreck (if no harm happen), yet it is a felony.**

"**If anyone convey secretly any of the goods, if it be the value of a nail, it is felony**".

Under those laws, if the mob on the beach made sure that no man, woman, cat or dog reached the shore alive, the salvor, even if caught with the goods, could say he was about to take it to the local authority and could then, at least, make some sort of claim for salvage.

The law was a clear invitation to murder, but the reference to luring a ship ashore by lights is an odd one. I can find no record of this happening in Devon, though it would hardly be in the laws unless it had happened. It sounds more like Cornwall, or even Hollywood, than South Hams! There is no doubt though about the looting of shipwrecks in this area.

Read the chapter on "Wrack" in a book written by Henry Hingeston in 1703. Mr.Hingeston was a Kingsbridge merchant and his book with the strange title - "A Dreadful Alarm upon the Clouds of Heaven mixed with Love" - contained "sundry Warnings and Admonitions to the Inhabitants...particularly to those of the Town of Kingsbridge in Devon and parts adjacent.."

About "wrack" he writes: "**I have been deeply Affected to see and feel how sweet the Report of a Shipwreck is to the Inhabitants of this Country, as well Professors as Profane; and what running there is on such Occasions, all other business thrown aside, and away to Wrack....**

"**Hearken a little: Suppose you were Cast away in a strange country, having much to do to save your Lives, but however you come safe ashore, and are in some Capacity of saving most, if not all your Goods, by some small assistance; but at the same time to prevent you from that, down comes a parcel of Fellows on you, that instead of Helping of you, take away all, and compassionate you no** more than Dogs, nay, if you have sav'd anything, they'll be forward to take it from you; but when they cannot do that, you being driven of Necessity to sell, they'll scarce give half, perhaps not a quarter its value. Pray what would you say of those folks? Have you not done as bad as all this? I conclude you cannot say no, except against your Knowledge. Nay, have you not done much worse? I say you have. Remember the Broad Cloth Slupe stranded in Bigbury Bay, Richly Laden..."

It sounds as though Mr.Hingeston had an interest in that ship! He gives no further clue to her name or place of wrecking, but it does give us an idea of what happened when a ship went on shore.

There is more detail about a later wreck, that of the Dutch galliott on Thurlestone Sands in 1753. To find out what happened we can still read today the letter of Mr.George Taylor to Sir William Courtenay, who owned the rights to wreck from Dartmouth to Bantham. Mr.Taylor was Sir William's agent and he wrote this letter to his master from his home in Totnes on January 16th, 1753:

"Honoured Sir,

I hope you, my lady and family, had a safe journey to Town, after such bad weather, as probably you had on your road.

I'm to acquaint you that last Wednesday night, about ten, a Hamburgh-Dutch galliott, burden about one hundred tons, laden with wine, brandy, coffee, indigo, and one bale of saffron, bound from Zante to Hamburgh, was stranded on Thurlestone sands, within the precinct of your Royalty.

Thursday morn I went thither to do what lay in my power to prevent the country from plundering her and to save the cargo, and have the pleasure to let your Honour know that more than three parts of four is so done.

The lost cable and anchor I've secured (as usual) for your use; but as to what share of the salvage (extracted from the expenses of saving) is due to you I'm at a loss to judge at, especially as the ship is not broke to pieces by the waves, and the master and men all saved, and not deemed wreck.

As your Honour is in Town you may advise what is most proper to be done by me for your interest. The Custom House officer of Plymouth, Dartmouth, and Salcombe all assisted in saving the goods. The cargo is valued at about £3,000. A great part of the goods are in the custody of Mr.Adams and others of your tenants.

A great part of the goods were saved Thursday and Friday from being plundered by my being there, on account of my acquaintance and knowing most of the persons then there; but Saturday evening there were not less than ten thousand people who came from remote parts in order to plunder the remainder of the cargo, which they had certainly done if the Plymouth official had not ordered a party of soldiers to attend, who opportunely came just as the mob was about to make a disturbance; by accident one of the ringleaders was killed, he being drunk and falling upon one of the soldier's bayonets fixed on the gun. This and other circumstances gave a damp to the rest of the rioters; and more goods have been saved out of this vessel than all the ships that have been stranded for fifty years past.

I am, your Honour's most faithful servant,

Geo. Taylor

P.S. I'm but just come home weary and tired, wet every day into the skin, but helping the distressed makes an atonement."

George Taylor sounds a dreadful creep, but his letter does give us some idea of how important a wreck was to everyone for miles around.

Foot Note: If you divert into the village of Thurlestone and walk up the village street, look at the beams over the windows of the thatched houses. Those lintels on the older houses are all made from shipwreck timber and have holes for wooden pegging in them. Decent wood beams cost a fortune in the days those houses were built and a shipwreck supplied them free as long as they were not claimed by the lord of the manor! At the time of the wreck, Mr.William Adams, who is described in the letter as looking after "a great part of the goods" from the ship, lived in a house, which is now Bromfield's shop, near the Village Inn.

13. GEORGE AND ANN
The Book Rocks, Thurlestone 1808

NO one knows why the Book Rocks, which show at low tide just to the west of Thurlestone Rock, got their name. One theory is that their name comes from the part they played in the drama which took place in the morning of October 23rd, 1808.

Then the boom and crack of gunfire filled the air and a small English merchantman strained across the bay with all sails set, heading for Hope. Ship on the run was the *George and Ann* of Exeter. Waterspouts from near-miss cannonballs gouted up on either side of her and Captain Hodder knew that one slightly better-aimed shot would mean capture and a long spell in a French prison for him and his crew. The ship racing along behind him was a French privateer, a chasse-maree, or coastal lugger, 65 feet long, carrying ten guns and a crew of over 70. This Frenchman was a three-master with the aft mast almost hanging out over the stern. Her large sails needed the big crew to handle them and her fastest speed was not when running directly before the wind - a failing which Captain Hodder was relying on to keep him ahead long enough to get into the shelter of Hope. The Frenchman, however, was still closing by using topsails on her racked-back masts.

But Hodder was a Kingsbridge man and knew these waters well. Realising that on his present course he would never reach Hope before being overhauled and boarded, he tried a desperate last ploy. The Book Rocks were still covered though the tide was going down. Gambling that the French captain lacked his local knowledge, he took the *George and Ann* right over the centre of the Books. He heard the French crew whoop in triumph - they had him now! But those sounds of triumph changed the next moment to cries of alarm, then the privateer struck hard and those tilted back masts came crashing down forwards.

But the English crew had no time to cheer. The tide had been ebbing longer than Hodder thought. His ship grated on a rock and the next moment they too were firmly aground on the centre group of the Books. And there the two enemies stuck only yards from each other. There is no record of what happened next, but the two ships were reported as total wrecks.

Foot Note:Do you think the name of that reef had something to do with those wrecks and "being brought to book"? Or do you think that the rocks were named after the brook, which runs under the footbridge you walked across near Thurlestone at the foot of South Milton Ley. The Ley shelters one of the largest reed beds in Devon and is an important bird sanctuary. It can be no coincidence that the brook emerges through the beach of Thurlestone Sands immediately opposite the rocks, which were probably known as the Brook Rocks, but got the "r" dropped during all the copying which went on in early days with one map-maker taking material shamelessly from his predecessor.

Thurlestone Sands, as you will see, are now a paradise for wind-surfers. Due to some silly politically correct interpretation of parochial boundaries, the National Trust to whom the land behind the beach belongs, will insist on calling them "South Milton Sands", but Thurlestone Sands they have been since Thurlestone Rock was named in the Domesday Book - and Thurlestone Sands is their proper name.

14. CHANTELOUPE.
Thurlestone Rock. 1772.

DID they murder the wife of Edmund Burke's brother when she was washed ashore on Thurlestone Sands? Did people from Thurlestone really cut off her ears for her earrings and chop off her fingers for her rings? That's the story, which has been part of the history of the area since the tale first surfaced in the early 1800s.

It always ends with the villains getting their just deserts like this..."They do say, m'dears, as how them what done it, all came to a bad end. None of 'em lasted no more than a year after they killed her. One of 'em went off his head an' ran into the sea. 'Nother hung hisself out the back of the

The Chanteloupe's cannon lie under the sand just a few feet from Thurlestone Rock. Here divers begin removing the sand and a cannon starts to emerge.

The divers use a water dredge to suck away more sand.

cot. And the third...well he were found dead up along Buckland way. Say his cart ran over hisself, but no one b'aint too sure bout that..."

The truth is not quite the same. On Wednesday, September 23, 1772, the wind came hard from the south. It blew so strong and grew so quickly that ships in the Channel ran for shelter. If they made it they were lucky, for that evening the wind shifted and something even stronger came howling in from the Atlantic.

First to feel the power of this great wind from the south-west were the Scilly Isles. Within a few hours, 14 ships had been lost within sight of St.Mary's. Caught far out to sea, the *Chanteloupe*, homeward bound from Grenada in the West Indies for London, ran before that wind up Channel with nearly all sails furled away.

The wind was behind her, all around her, and well ahead of her. At Ramsgate, it caught two ships and flung them ashore, one on each side of the jetty. A third was not even that lucky and she was described as "now ready to be swallowed up by the Goodwin Sands; the sea so rough that no one durst venture to their assistance". Near North Foreland, a large West Indiaman was driven on to the rocks, and when the wind curled round into the Thames Estuary, boats were smashed and driven ashore as though models on a pond.

That night houses were blown down in London's Spitalfield and so was one wall of the Fleet Prison. Trees in the parks and in Holloway were ripped up by the roots. All over the City windows caved in and roofs complete with slates were whirled away. Those who came out in the morning and breathed a sigh of relief that their homes were intact, were premature.

That day the wind came back again and now it was even stronger. Bridges all over the country collapsed and land anywhere near a river flooded. At sea the *Catherine* from Norway to Dublin actually had all her masts ripped out before she sank, though a few of her crew were saved. The *Phoenix* of Captain Hanin struggled into Plymouth for shelter, but found none and was driven on shore in the Cattewater.

Now somewhere off Cornwall, Captain Michael Tobin struggled to keep his *Chanteloupe* afloat, but squall by squall the wind pushed him on past the Eddystone. In London more buildings fell to the ground.

By the evening it was blowing a full hurricane. Nothing could stand against it. A Dutch ship, laden with wine and sugar, was wrecked on the Chesil Beach. All the crew, but one, were pounded to death by the surf. At Portland two ships were driven off their anchors in the Roads and never seen again.

At the same time that evening of September 24, 1772, under a sky as black as though it was midnight, Captain Tobin lost his fight to save the *Chanteloupe*. In gaps in the smoking spray, he saw the shore, even fancied that he could make out people on it when suddenly a huge rock with the wind howling through a hole in it and making a noise like a giant fog-horn, raced towards him.

For a moment Tobin thought they would end up on top of it, but then his ship ground to a halt just in front of it. The next wave slewed him round broadside to the shore and the following ones started breaking the ship to pieces.

It is unlikely that Captain Tobin knew where he was. But his ship was, in fact, skewered on the rocks just in front of Thurlestone Rock, that strange stone, which is noted in the

Local divers Neville Oldham and Kendall McDonald examine the cannon after it was lifted with airbags and brought ashore near Hope Cove's old lifeboat slipway. This cannon can now be seen outside The Thurlestone Hotel.

Domesday Book as "thirled" or pierced, and which sits in front of the eastern end of Thurlestone Sands. The wind at the time of the wreck was blowing almost straight on shore and in those conditions today the hole in the rock creates a huge moaning whine which carries for miles inshore.

What happened then at the wreck of the *Chanteloupe* depends a great deal on who is telling the story. If you rely on Kingsbridge folk, such as Sarah Prideaux Fox, whose book was published in 1864, nearly one hundred years after the wreck, the folk roundabout were a rotten lot. In her book, she described the affair like this:

"About the year 1772, a vessel returning from the West Indies was wrecked in Bigbury Bay; all on board perished with the exception of one man, who was rescued by the humanity of a farmer, who lived in the neighbourhood, of the name of Hannaford.

Amongst the other passengers there was a lady, who it is supposed, seeing the desperate state of the vessel, put on her richest gems and apparel, with the hope that if she were washed towards the shore, those who found her might be induced to save her. She was thrown by the sea on the beach, and they say that life was not extinct when she reached it, but the savage people (from the adjacent villages) who were anxiously waiting for the wreck, seized and stripped her of her clothes; they even cut off some of her fingers, and mangled her ears in their impatience to secure her jewels, and then left her miserably to perish."

Other reports in later years improved on this by saying that the woman was Mrs. Burke, wife of the brother of Edmund Burke, the famous orator, and that the three men, who did the dreadful deed, did not realise that she was still alive until they saw the blood spurting from her severed fingers, and then it was too late so they buried her in the sand of the beach. But the next day, a dog belonging to a man described as "Jan Whiddon's father" dug the body up and the local gentry had the body reburied in a Christian manner. A Kingsbridge family were said to have treasured a piece of lace from her dress for many years after the wreck.

But even these tales were improved on by one which added Edmund Burke coming down from London and asking nasty questions about the death of his sister-in-law. He went back to London, according to that storyteller, no wiser than he came as the local village "mafia" had ordered no one to talk.

However all this gossip pales when you see a report by an eyewitness of the wreck. This appeared in the Exeter Flying Post on October 9th, 1772 and is part of a letter from a Customs Officer at Dartmouth to a friend in Exeter:

"Your Favour came duly to Hand, and would have been sooner answered, but am just returned from a Barbarian Country, by which I mean that I have been five Days absent from Dartmouth to the Westward about twenty Miles, on a most melancholy Affair.

"A Ship about 300 Tuns, from the Granadoes for London, laden with Sugar, Coffee, Rum, Madiera Wine, &c. was wrecked in Bigbury Bay last Week, and out of twenty Persons only one was saved, which was the second Mate, and he, for some Days, remained quite stupified. There were seven Passengers on board, the principal of whom were John Burke, Esq, (who was a Man of Immense Fortune; he sold a Plantation a few Days before his Departure for 32,000 pounds and has a Brother in London); Timothy Plip, Esq; and his Lady, Natives of Ireland - The Ship by all Accounts had great Treasure on board.

"There were twelve of the Bodies washed on Shore during my Stay, and the inhuman Country People strip'd them quite naked, and left them on the Rocks. - I leave you to judge the dismal, shocking Sights we beheld, indeed I cannot describe it; I should much rather have been excused from going, but as an Officer of the Customs, the Duty called me.

"It was really dangerous to be among such Wretches - There were between 4 and 5,000 Persons assembled, most of whom, for the Sake of a little Pelf, would be guilty of the greatest Acts of Cruelty: I do assure you that I could wish to see one half of them hanged on the Cliffs, for Example to the rest. The Lady was seen hanging by one Arm to a Rock, and no Person would go to save her, tho' there was not the least Danger: She was with Child and near her Time. - Those that washed on Shore we took Care to have buried in Thurlestone Church-yard."

Foot Note: Though there was no cutting off of ears and fingers in that report, it hardly paints a happy picture of a shipwreck in the South Hams. You can see at once where the story of the woman comes from and that of Edmund Burke. Edmund's brother was not the John Burke in the wreck, though as his brother Richard was once H.M.Collector of Customs and Receiver General of Revenues in Grenada and had large land-dealings there, the man in the wreck is probably a relative. There seems to be no record of the burials in Thurlestone Churchyard, though a cannon raised from the wreck by divers in recent years can be seen well displayed close to the entrance to the Thurlestone Hotel.

At full low spring tides it is possible to clamber out over the rocks to Thurlestone Rock itself. The wreck lies under the sand in a gully about ten feet from the eastern edge of the Rock. **Take great care the rocks are always extremely slippery with seaweed.**

It is interesting to find in some old records of the wreck that Thurlestone Rock was then known as the "King's Gate". The Rock is 30ft high and 40ft long. The hole in it is 20ft high and ten feet wide.

15. OREGON. Off Thurlestone Sands, 1890

THE *Oregon* of 801 tons, a three-masted steel-hulled sailing ship of Dundee, doesn't seem to have been lucky with her choice of pilot.

Her captain, Albert Lowe, brought her safely without such help round Cape Horn and across the Atlantic from Iquique, Chile, to Falmouth, Cornwall. His orders were to take on a pilot there before continuing his voyage with a cargo of nitrate of soda to Newcastle-on-Tyne.

In spite of the pilot's help, in the dark and heavy rain of the evening of December 18, 1890, the *Oregon* struck The Books, the reef of rocks almost directly off Thurlestone Sands, which shows well before low water (see Wreck No.13). Captain Lowe immediately put her about, got clear and headed out to sea.

He had no sooner done so, than he knew from the feel of her that she was rapidly filling with water. The leak was so bad that he ordered the crew to abandon her. The first boat lowered was swamped by the high seas, but the second was successfully launched. In the pitch dark, they drifted for twelve hours before making out the land. In fact, it wasn't until 6am in the morning that "guided by the light from a labourer's lantern on the shore", according to The Times, "the sailors succeeded in reaching the fishing village

The Oregon today. This underwater photograph of part of the wreck shows how she has collapsed. The lignum vitae blocks of her rigging can be seen clearly.

Report of the wreck of the Theodor in the Kingsbridge Gazette of Saturday, February 21, 1874.

WRECK AT THURLESTONE.

GALLANT RESCUE BY COASTGUARD MEN.

On Saturday evening a calamitous wreck occurred close by Thurlestone rock; a German brigantine, the Theodore of Hamburg; 160 tons; laden with cotton seed and sundry dye-woods, from Barcelona for Hamburg, being driven ashore, and she now lies embedded in the sands. It appears that the vessel left her port of clearance with captain, mate, and four hands, and experienced on her way very heavy weather, which increased in violence on her entrance into the chops of the channel. During a storm on Wednesday last the mate, assisted by two of the men was midships, endeavouring to secure the boat, which by the violence of the waves had been knocked out of her chalks, when a heavy sea struck her, carrying away the two men from the mate's side, and likewise bowsprit, mainsail, foresail, stay-sail, and all gear attached, with starboard anchor, and fifteen fathoms of chain. The mate then going aft to report to the captain, who had been at the wheel, found him missing, and sought him in vain over the ship, the same wave which carried off the other men, having likewise carried off their leader. Under these trying circumstances, the mate took the command of the vessel; but the chronometer being run down, and as no sights had been obtainable since Tuesday, on Saturday the ship made Bolt Tail, the mate, who had been at the wheel for four successive days and nights without rest, mistaking it for the Lizard Point.

The news of a vessel being in distress was conveyed to the Chief Officer of the coast guard at two o'clock. The ship was then in the act of wearing round to go on another tack ahead to westward, when, after proceeding down the bay for some distance, the wind veered more westerly, and the mate, seeing of Hope, where they were treated with great kindness."

The *Oregon* sank as soon as the second boat had been launched and is now upright, but rusting away in 100 feet of water. She is often visited by divers, who have recovered some of her rigging blocks. bow. They are of lignum vitae, which polishs up beautifully even after its long stay underwater.

16. THEODOR
By Thurlestone Rock, 1874.

THOUGH the storm which had swept the South Hams during Saturday, February 14, 1874, was one of the main topics of conversation, in Kingsbridge itself, the scandal concerning Mr.Bourne and Mrs.Heimer took priority over everything, even whether Disraeli would abolish income tax if he beat Gladstone at the forthcoming General Election.

In the Kingsbridge Gazette of that very morning, an advertisement appeared which gave a new impetus to the Bourne-Heimer affair, provoking talk of a duel no less! The advertisement took the form of a letter to Mr.Furneaux Heimer of Stokenham, which was dated February 11th, 1874, and read:

" *Sir,*

Having at the Market Ordinary, at the King's Arms Hotel, on Wednesday, the 15th day of October last, inadvertently made use of an observation reflecting on the character of your wife in consequence of a rumour from an unreliable source, I beg to withdraw such observation and to apologise, and to express my regret for having made it, and you are at liberty to make any use of this letter.

I am, Sir,

Yours obediently,

ROBERT BOURNE.*"*

Presumably everyone for miles around knew what Mr.Bourne called Mrs.Heimer. However, it seems unlikely now that we shall ever know what he said.

But while the locals gossiped as their windows rattled and the rain lashed down on their righteousness, there were others who had no time for such things, they were more concerned with staying alive amid the huge waves those same winds had created out at sea.

The German brigantine *Theodor* of 160 tons, laden with cotton seed and dye-woods, was well off course as she battled her way from Barcelona in Venezuela towards Hamburg, Germany. Her voyage had gone wrong from the very beginning.

Storm had followed storm. When she reached the entrance to the Channel, the winds had gone beserk. Fighting to keep the ship afloat were the captain, Claus Stehr, the mate and four hands.

On Wednesday, February 11th, the mate together with two crewmen dragged themselves amidships to try and secure the ship's boat which had been knocked clean out of her chocks, and was in danger of going over the side. The men heaved and strained, but were making little impression when a huge wave struck the ship and carried away not only the boat, but the two men from the mate's side. The same wave took away the bowsprit, the mainsail, the forestay sail, all the attached gear and the starboard anchor with 15 fathoms of chain.

The mate went to report to the captain, who had been at the wheel. When he got there, he found the wheel spinning aimlessly and no sign of the captain. At first the mate could not believe it and searched everywhere for the captain until finally he knew that the same wave had carried away the captain too.

The mate was now in command. But the ship he commanded was lost. The ship's chronometer had stopped, no sextant sights had apparently been taken since the storm started and he had little idea of where he was. Still he took the wheel and stayed with it for two successive days and nights until he saw what he thought was Lizard Point. It was in fact Bolt Tail.

The mate put the ship into another tack and when Stoke Point loomed up, he began to realise he was embayed. He tacked again and lost ground against the westerly gale.

By now *Theodor* had been seen from the land - by Joseph Urell, Chief Officer of the Hope Coastguard. It was just on two o'clock. The nearest lifeboat was the one at Salcombe, but Urell knew there was little chance of that boat making it even if she could fight her way over Salcombe Bar and along the Bolt in the teeth of the wind.

It was madness to try and launch any boat at Hope. The surf pounded the beach and the waves were so high that they looked bound to capsize any boat which tried to get out. But Joseph Urell asked his men to try. The report of the wreck says: "**Mr. Urell - although the task seemed a hopeless one and death seemed almost certain - most gallantly resolved to endeavour to save the lives of the helpless ones. Appealing to his men, the noble reply of the chief boatman was 'Where you go, I'll go' and of the others 'We'll follow";** but still one man was wanting, and a fisherman most heroically and courageously offered his services to pull the vacant oar, and these men - a forlorn hope - set out on their self-imposed mission of mercy." We know that fisherman was James Ash, presumably all the others were coastguards.

Eye-witnesses of the time said that they had never seen such breakers in the bay and even if there was some shelter for the rescue boat inside Hope Cove, there was certainly no protection from the howling wind further out at sea. How the rowers managed to get close to the *Theodor*, it is difficult to imagine, particularly as she was now off Thurlestone. But they did close with her; one moment high in the air on top of a wave above her, the next looking up at the hull of the wallowing brigantine.

As brigantines go, the *Theodor* was not large, 120-feet-long with a 26-foot beam, but these small vessels were common on the long ocean routes in the middle of the 19th century. It was only at the beginning of the 1900's that they began to disappear. Until then the type was very popular with shipowners - smaller than a barque, cheaper to build, cheap to run, and able to get into most small ports.

But now it looked as though the *Theodor* had seen her last port. The shore got closer every moment. Urell's men tried again and again to hold her close enough for the crew to jump. Finally, the two seamen made it, but the mate refused to leave his ship.

It was only when Urell produced his pistol and threatened to shoot the man unless he abandoned ship, that the mate jumped and landed sprawling amid the oarsmen.

With the extra weight aboard making rowing even more difficult the boat somehow got back into Hope to the "ringing cheers " of those who had watched the rescue from the shore.

The wind now had *Theodor* to itself and drove her straight towards the shore. Within minutes the ship was amid the rocks close to Thurlestone Rock and then was carried on to the sands to the west. She did not stay whole for long and soon her cargo of cotton seed and dye-wood was spread all along Thurlestone Sands.

The dye-wood was a kind of sandalwood, which, when soaked in alcohol, produced a bright crimson dye. Some of that wood has been used in at least one Thurlestone cottage as lintels over the windows.

Joseph Urell was awarded the RNLI silver medal and all the rescuers were rewarded. But the rescue and the wreck did more than that. They were directly responsible for a lifeboat being stationed at Hope and operational from 1878 to 1930.

Foot Note: The RNLI was asked by local residents to station a boat at Hope and the station was approved on March 1, 1877. Six months later the Freemasons of England donated £4,000 to provide and endow two lifeboat stations. This gift was to record their pleasure that their Grand Master, the Prince of Wales, had returned safely from a tour of India. The money provided a station at Clacton, Essex as well as the one in Hope Cove. The Earl of Devon gave the land on which the lifeboat house was built. The lifeboat house, complete with inscriptions, now privately owned, is still there at the foot of the coast path where it comes down from Bolt Tail into Hope Cove. The slipway in front of the lifeboat house was first used for a real rescue by Hope Cove's first lifeboat, *Alexandra*, a 35-

The tug Empire Harry impaled on Beacon Point.

footer, ten-oared, self-righting craft, at 8.30 a.m. on January 18,1887, when she went to help the crew of the *Halloween*, wrecked in Sewer Mill Cove (see Wreck No.28).

17. EMPIRE HARRY
Beacon Point, Hope, 1945.

TUGS were in short supply at the start of the Second World War and demand increased as the war went on. Tugs were needed to try to pull torpedo or bomb victims into shallow water or repair yards. Tugs were needed to marshal ships into convoys. Tugs were needed to tow the Mulberry Harbour units for D-Day. And after that more tugs were needed to haul barges laden with war supplies across the Channel to keep the Allied armies pushing forward into Germany. And tugs had to keep on doing so to keep the armies supplied even after the war in Europe was over.

To carry out all these tasks, Britain had embarked on a major tug building programme soon after the outbreak of war. This was part of a major building programme of ships of all types. All were given the prefix "Empire" to their names. Tugs were built in groups to standard patterns. The Goole Shipbuilding and Repairing Company built four of the Larch Class in their yard on the River Humber. One of those tugs launched on October 12,1942 and completed for Naval service in March,1943, was the *Empire Harry*.

Like her three sisters - *Empire Larch, Empire Oak*, and *Empire Rupert* - she was 135 feet long with a beam of 30 and a draught of 16 and she had 1,100 hp.steam engines. Empire Harry took part in the D-Day landings and survived the war. But only just. She was towing two U.S.Army barges from Falmouth to Antwerp on June 6,1945, when a Force 8 gale from the south-west hit her as she crossed Bigbury Bay. Though it sounds an impossible mix, with that gale came thick fog. Despite her powerful engines, the wind and the drag of the two lighters pushed her on to the rocks of Beacon Point, which suddenly loomed up out of the fog.

When she struck, the barges snapped free, or were cast off, and they broke up further along the coast to the east. The 19 crew of the tug were rescued by the Salcombe lifeboat and the tug became a total wreck.

Foot Note: Beacon Point juts out from the coast just half-a-mile along the South-West Coast Path from Hope to Thurlestone Sands and is said to have been the site of a beacon warning of the Armada in 1588. It seems an unlikely place for such a beacon. It is more likely that it was where a beacon was lit to help guide the fishermen of Hope back home in bad weather.

At low tide you can see boiler of the *Empire Harry* about 400 yards out. There are plates and ribs closer in to the Point.

SECTION THREE – Hope to Bolt Head

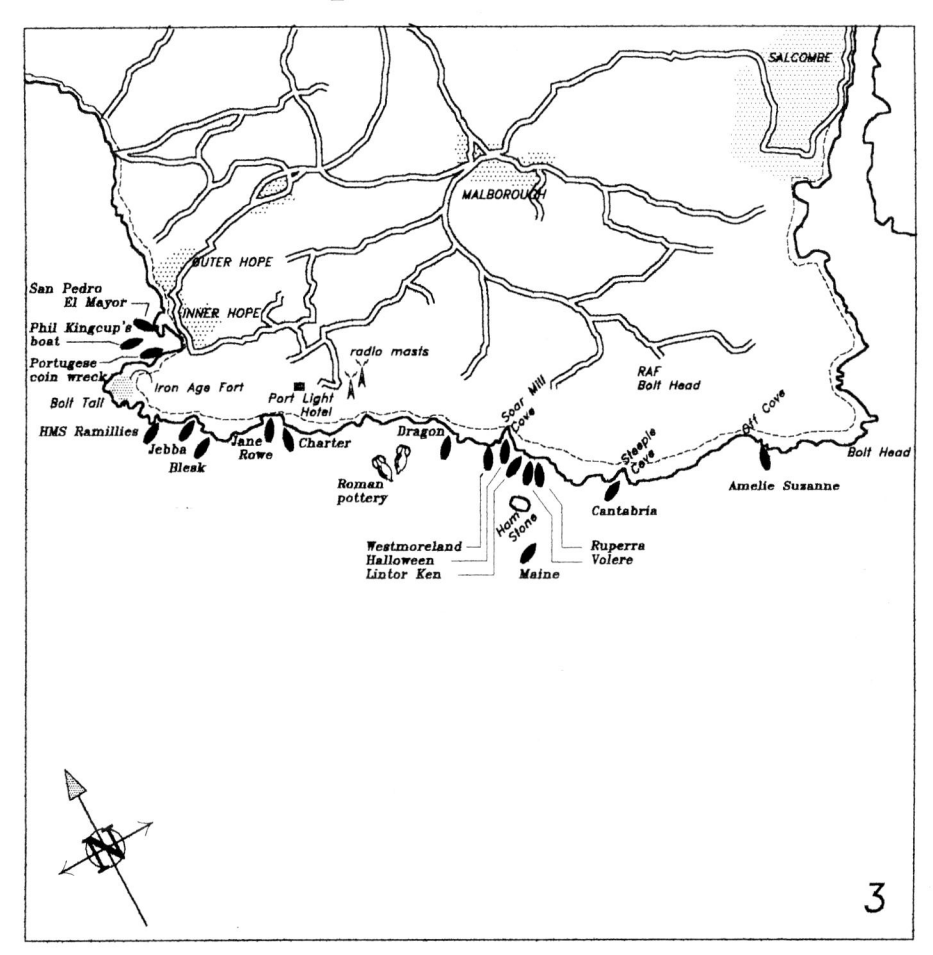

FROM Hope Cove, where in the mid-1800s as many as 60 vessels could be seen sheltering for days at a time from easterly gales, the path climbs up to Bolt Tail (there is an alternative route from the thatched cottages of the original village, now called Inner Hope, which joins the main path near Whitechurch cove). Ahead of you now, to Bolt Head, are five miles of the most spectacular cliff walking in Britain.

At tip of the Tail itself are the earthworks of an Iron Age fort, probably occupied before 200AD. Near the tail but further to the east is a coastguard watch-house.

There are many wrecks reported along this stretch of coast and probably more which died unknown and unseen. Some very early wrecks were victims of the cliffs. Local fishermen say they have pulled up shards of pottery very like Roman amphora fragments, particularly in the area off Bolberry Down. Coins have been found nearby.

Places to note along the cliffs are:

Easton's Mine. If you look seaward and down to the west from the first stile on Bolberry Down, you'll see a chalybeate spring coming out of the cliff about half-way down. That's where the entrance to the mine is. Don't try to climb down. It's very dangerous without ropes. John Easton of Kingsbridge brought in Cornish miners to dig out copper, but they found only iron pyrites. The miners had fallen in love with some lovelies in Hope and when they went back to Cornwall on leave brought back real copper ore and "salted" the mine so they could stay on in Hope. But John Easton rumbled them in the end and back to Cornwall they went!

Bolberry Down is the open land stretching to the west from the Port Light and it was here on May 29, 1768 that the Kingsbridge Races were first held. However, in order to avoid the attentions of the law and the taxes, the races were called the "Kingsbridge Annual Diversions" and prizes were held below £50. They were staged on the Down for three years each June and were then moved to land belonging to Middle Sewer farm, an ancient building now abandoned as a living place, which you can reach by a footpath leading off the Heritage coast path where it crosses the Warren between Steeple and Off Coves. In 1782, the races were moved to East Allington and then the next year became Totnes Races.

The Port Light Hotel, known for its crab sandwiches and good pub grub, was originally the clubhouse of a nine-hole golf links on Bolberry Down, which was opened in 1909 and lasted for only a few years. During the war, the Port Light was used as dining and recreation rooms for the Bolt Tail radar station, which was manned mainly by W.A.A.Fs. Some remains of the radar station itself - concrete blocks - can be seen today close on the seaward side of the path to the south-west behind the Port Light building.

Ralph's Hole is a cave in the sheer cliff face behind the Port Light Hotel. Do not attempt to climb down to Ralph's Hole, the cliff falls sheer from its entrance hundreds of feet to the sea. It is an empty dreary cave some 20 feet deep, by seven wide and eight high. It is named after a fellow called Ralph, who in the 1700s kept the "catchpoles" (sheriff's officers) successfully at bay with a pitchfork from the narrow entrance when they tried to arrest him.

Those three huge radio masts near the Port Light are part of the Decca Navigation System. Further on, notice the medieval system of using slate slabs to divide up the fields beside the path.

Pixy Dance. A piece of rough ground near Bolberry Down marked by two very large stones of equal size. The fairies (or in Devon the pixies) are often seen here. It is their principal resort in the whole of Devonshire. The Devon pixies are said to be the souls of heathens who died before the coming of Christianity and so are "not good enough for heaven, but too good for hell" so they are doomed to wander for evermore. Walkers who are bothered by them - they make their victims dance with them and have the same effect as alcohol.- have only to turn their pockets inside out for the pixies to disappear!

Cathole Cliff is said to have been named after a colony of wild cats which lived there, but there is a suggestion that as the old word "Catte" meant ship (e.g. the Cattewater at Plymouth and the Kattegat - ship gate) it could mean "Ship-hole" and mark the site of a shipwreck.

Lantern Rock is so called because those with a good imagination can picture it as lantern-shaped.

Soar Mill Cove (Sewer Mill Cove) has some strange tales attached to it. In the 17th century and later, it was firmly believed that a cave on the eastern side of the cove was just the start of one which went right through to exit at Bull Hole, Splat Cove, which you'll find near South Sands, Salcombe. They said too that a black bull which had entered the cave at one end had emerged pure white at the other!

The use of the name "Soar" seems a fairly modern creation to avoid the word "sewer", but maps and old documents prior to the early 1900s all persist with Sewer. In fact "sewer" was a corruption of the Anglo-Saxon "sae-ware" meaning sea-dwellers and so probably indicates the site of an early settlement. The old form - "Sewer" - has been used in this book where appropriate.

R.A.F. Bolt Head, which had two airstrips, and was used as a "last resort" landing field for aircraft damaged over France and for fighter sweeps in support of the Allied Armies in Normandy, was on land behind the Warren between Higher Soar Farm and East Soar. It was operational from 1941 to April,1945.

18. SAN PEDRO EL MAYOR.
Hope Cove, 1588.

THE only Spanish Armada ship known to have been wrecked in England is believed to have struck the Shippen Rock in the centre of Hope Cove on October 28,1588. Certainly we know the *San Pedro el Mayor* (St.Peter the Great) was wrecked at Hope on that day, but the local claim that she hit the Shippen Rock in a south-westerly gale - Shippen...Ship-on..get it? - is perhaps too simple to be true.

But details of the *San Pedro*'s last voyage are well recorded. Her captain was Francisco de Silva, and despite the fact that she carried 30 iron cannon, she was no fighting ship. She was one of the Squadron of Urcas, which were the transports and supply ships of the Armada, and was fitted out as a hospital ship, according to the inventory made at Lisbon on May 20,1588. Commanding 100 soldiers aboard was Diego de Allier and the controller of the hospital was Rodriguo de Calderon.

The urca squadron was commanded by Juan Gomez de Medina from his flagship, the *Gran Grifon*. His urcas, including the 580-ton *San Pedro*, were safely inside the great crescent-shaped battle formation of the Armada when the first skirmishes took place off Plymouth on July 21,1588. Skirmish is too light a word for those early battles as by Wednesday August 3, the Armada galleons were taking a terrible pounding from English cannon. One Spanish ship, for example, was seen to have blood running out of the

An engraving of the time shows the crescent formation adopted by the Spanish Armada as it moved up Channel.
The San Pedro El Mayor is one of the ships in the centre safely inside the wings of the fleet.

deck scupper pipes into the sea. And the commander of the urca squadron didn't escape unscathed. He was unwise enough to let his flagship, *Gran Grifon*, get behind one of the tips of the Spanish formation.

Drake swooped with all sails bent to take advantage of the light wind near Portland Bill. The *Gran Grifon* was too late to get back to shelter. Drake put *Revenge* on a broadside course, gave her every gun, then came about and gave her the other broadside. Then raked her again from "half musket shot" distance as he raced across her stern. Seventy men on *Gran Grifon* were either killed or wounded and her decks were described as slippery with blood. There were 70 cannon balls in her hull before she struggled back into formation. Some of the wounded were transferred into the *San Pedro*. The *Gran Grifon* was repaired at Gravelines. The Armada sailed on until fireships and the weather forced them to flee through the North Sea and up to the very tip of Scotland.

Now the only way home was round Scotland and down the west coast of Ireland. The *San Pedro* lurched on after her commander in the *Gran Grifon*. But on August 20, when the Armada passed between Ronaldsay and Fair Isle, neither the *San Pedro* or the *Gran Grifon* was with them. Fierce squalls had split the lumbering transports from the main force. *Gran Grifon* had five ships with her, but the *San Pedro* was not one of them. She was alone in the huge seas, being pushed hither and thither by the gales which followed one another in a relentless sequence.

One of those gales put paid to the *Gran Grifon*. She was wrecked on Fair Isle, but Juan Gomez de Medina and 300 men survived.

The Duke of Medina Sidonia, commanding the Armada, had ordered his captains not to seek shelter in Irish ports. He feared that any which did would meet with no quarter. Some defied his orders later. The *San Pedro* was in a bad way. One report said that her water barrels were foul and the water so stinking and full of growths that they had to strain it through their teeth to get any liquid at all. And there is evidence that she too defied orders and went into the port of Vicey in County Kerry to get fresh water.

But she had to sail again. And she did - into more gales. The continual struggle against the winds took its toll of soldiers and sailors alike and fewer and fewer men had the strength to work the ship. Some idea of what it was like aboard comes in a report that some of the more seriously wounded drowned in the water which swilled back and forth below decks.

Finally she was out of control. The winds blew her before them and after a three-month voyage, she was back where her troubles had started - off Plymouth. With not enough men able to set sails, a south-westerly gale now headed her straight towards the very heart of her enemies, Plymouth Sound. Then the wind shifted slightly and she came into Bigbury Bay. On and on and then, as though committing suicide, straight into Hope Cove and on to the rocks. Huge seas began to break over her.

If the Spaniards aboard were too weak to handle the ship, they were apparently not too weak to set about saving themselves and, in some cases, their belongings. We know this because of a letter in the Calendar of State Papers (Domestic) for 1588 in the Public Record Office. The letter writer was George Cary, who was Deputy-Lieutenant of Devon. He had been staying at Plymouth when the news of the wreck reached him. He rode for Hope straight away. What he found and did about it is in his letter to the Privy Council, dated November 5th, 1588, which he wrote when he got back to his home at Cockington, near Torquay:

"...And during my abode there, having understanding that one of the Spanish fleet was cast on shore at a place called Hope and the great pilfering and spoils that the country people made, I rode thither and took order for the restoring and rehaving again of all such things as either by search or inquiry I could find out and have put the same in inventory. And took order, for the orderly saving of the rest, as weather would give leave, to have the same on land, appointing two head constables to attend that service, and they and others to keep several inventories.

"The ship is a hulk, and called St.Peter the Great, one of those two ships appointed for the hospital of the whole Navy. She is in burden, as they say, 550 tons, but I think not so much.

"The ship is not to be recovered; she lieth on a rock, and full of water to her upper decks. They confess that there were put into her, at her coming out of Spain, thirty mariners, one hundred soldiers, fifty appertaining to the hospital. There are now remaining about 140, or thereabouts.

"There was put into her as much drugs and pothecary stuff as came to 6,000 ducats, of which I think there will come little good of the same, the weather such as none could get aboard. There has been some plate and certain ducats rifled and spoiled at their first landing, both from their persons and out of their chests.

"The ship, I think, will prove of no great value; the ordnance is all iron, and no brass; their ground tackle all spent, save only one new cable. There are no men of account in the ship, soldiers and such as have risen by service, and bestowed all their wealth in this action".

Cary's statement about the number aboard suggest that 40 of her complement had gone and it sounds as though none of the sick or wounded aboard had survived. It also seems clear from his letter that some had got ashore with their chests and so must have used either boat or raft.

At this time Hope village was a few cottages, which survive today as Inner Hope. There was little place to keep the survivors of the wreck and 120 of them were crammed into one building in the locality, probably a barn, and were given some food and generally treated kindly by the villagers. Twenty officers were kept apart. Ten were sent into Kingsbridge. Cary himself took the apothecary and the surgeon into his home at Cockington. The remaining eight officers were taken to Ilton Castle, a mansion which then stood on the west side of the Salcombe estuary midway between Kingsbridge and Salcombe, and was the residence of Sir William Courtenay, the third Earl of Devon and High Sheriff of Devonshire, who was later to marry Sir Francis Drake's widow.

The prisoners then waited to hear what was to happen to them. They did not have to wait long. All were to be executed. Fortunately for the Spaniards, this order was quickly countermanded, though it was to be as long as five years before the last prisoner was ransomed and allowed home to Spain.

Foot Note: When you come down from Bolt Tail to Hope Cove the first building you will see is the old Lifeboat House with a slipway in front of it. If the tide is out and you go on to the beach there, keep your eyes open, particularly after a storm. For this is where some of the survivors of the *San Pedro* undoubtedly came ashore. Remember Cary's letter..."There has been some plate and certain ducats rifled and spoiled at their first landing, both from their persons and out of their chests..." Several of those "ducats" have been found over the years. They bear on one side the Maltese cross and on the other Philip of Spain's coat of arms surmounted by a royal crown. All have been found on this side of the cove.

This tiny pewter travelling cup was for giving communion to the sick. It was found crushed into a crevice in the Shippen Rock, Hope Cove and probably came from the San Pedro.

In 1990, local diver Stephen George found an Elizabethan-period pewter cup crushed into a crevice of the Shippen rock. The little pewter cup is described by experts as a travelling communion cup used by priests visiting the sick. It seems likely to have come from the Armada hospital ship.

To see other relics from the wreck a diversion from the path into Thurlestone will bring you to the Village Inn. Go into the saloon bar - excellent pub grub - where a notice will draw your attention to the great blackened old beams to the right of the main door. These are said to be from the St.Peter the Great.

In the Cookworthy Museum, at the top of Fore Street in Kingsbridge, you can see a Spanish helmet, which undoubtedly came from the wreck. There used to be some armour with it, but that now seems to have disappeared. The armour was found in the wall of St.Andrew's Church in the nearby village of Aveton Gifford during repairs in 1800. A strange place for it to be found? Not really. Back to Cary's letter again..."I rode thither and took order for the

This Spanish helmet from the wreck can be seen in the Cookworthy Museum, Fore Street, Kingsbridge.

them good sport. A man hunt was so much better than chasing foxes! He was only saved by the local gentry and then probably because they thought he was worth more alive in ransom money than just one day's sport.

We know that this wreck took place in Hope Cove. An old report of the wreck reads:

"At a later date a foreign ship went upon the rocks, and the inhabitants of the village were soon aboard. Having found there a Roman Catholic priest, they concluded he was a Jesuit, come as in Elizabeth's time to conspire against the government of the country, so they locked him up in the cabin and sent for the Malborough dogs - that is the local pack of hounds - to hunt him about the country, this being a form of insult offered in former days to unpopular people. The unfortunate man was saved from this outrage by the intervention of the local gentry."

Foot Note: It may, of course, be just a coincidence, but the next rock to the east of the Shippen (see Wreck No.18) has been known for centuries as the Old Priest!

restoring and rehaving again of all such things...appointing two head constables to attend that service..." What a panic to get rid of any loot there must have been after that. The wreck now belonged to the Crown and anyone caught with stolen Crown property would be likely to be hanged. A hole in a Church wall would have been as good a place as any to hide the evidence of such a dreadful crime!

19. PORTUGUESE COIN WRECK
Hope Cove, 1656.

As soon as the people of Hope had got aboard this ship from the rocks on which she was wrecked, they ransacked her. In the course of their looting, they discovered a Roman Catholic priest. Memories of the Armada were still strong, so they locked him in a cabin and sent for the local hounds. They thought he would give

These Portuguese cruzados were found under the sand at Hope. Picture: Roy Smallpage

The Portuguese wreck is probably the source of other silver coins found under the sands of Hope Cove. Like the ones from the *San Pedro el Mayor*, these coins were found at the eastern end of the Cove. In fact, most of them were uncovered when the lifeboat slipway was being repaired in 1912. However, any idea that these had come from the Armada ship was counted out immediately by the fact that they were cruzados of King John IV of Portugal, who reigned from 1640 to 1656.

20. PHIL KINGCUP'S BOAT
Hope, 1880.

IN these days of duty-free shops on car ferries running daily to Cherbourg and Roscoff, it is amusing to think that ships from Devon using those same courses more than two hundred years before were also operating a duty-free service.

For there was so much smuggling going on that it is accepted as fact that more rum and brandy were smuggled into Devon and Cornwall in the 1700's than came in legally to the Port of London.

Smuggling was rife in the South Hams - and easy - until the proper policing of the coast in the 1830's when a better coastguard system was introduced. But more coastguards, better trained and better paid, did not stop the smuggling.

In fact, so much smuggling went on that there are reports of farmers,"on taking out their horses to work in the fields in the morning, to find them in a state of inexplicable exhaustion..." Well, no doubt that is what the farmers told the Revenuemen, but only a very simple Revenueman would believe it!

In the early part of the 19th century, there were three lines of defence against the smugglers. There were the Revenue cutters, which boarded ships at sea and searched for contraband. Then there were the Preventative boats, which searched coastal waters, inlets and coastal creeks. And thirdly, there were the Riding Officers, who were mounted and armed to deal with "runs" on land.

In the South Hams the locals talked not of kegs of brandy, but of "tubs" and "ankers". An "anker" held eight gallons; a "tub" was four.

There was a lot of money to be made. A tub of brandy cost a little over 16s in France or the Channel Islands in the mid-1700's. Duty in Britain would be about 32s. But a smuggled tub was yours for 25s no questions asked.

At that time, the boats from Bantham, Salcombe, the Yealm and Plymouth were calling so regularly at Guernsey for cargos of spirits and tobacco, salt, silks and brocades that they could almost have published a timetable. Certainly they took orders for goods. However, in 1767, Guernsey and Jersey were taken out of the smuggler's top ten ports of call by the establishment of Customs there. As a result the illicit trade simply moved to Roscoff in France. The French were delighted and, in 1769, made it a free port.

Nat Cleverly, a Bantham smuggler, was one who would work the port of Roscoff in France. In one period of 12 days, he was one of nine South Hams boats which left Roscoff with 850 tubs aboard between them. At four gallons a tub that's a lot of booze. Amazingly, during the Napoleonic Wars, English, Scots and Irish merchants were allowed to operate warehouses in Roscoff to supply the smugglers. Napoleon, you see, had this theory that every smuggled tub was another blow to the British ability to pay her troops to wage war on him!

Running cargoes from Roscoff or Cherbourg was all right in fine weather, but a very different matter in a winter south-westerly gale.

It was a gale like that which brought to an end the smuggling career of Philip Kingcup of Hope. Here is how the wreck was reported by a smuggler, known only by his initials of "R.H.":

"That's true about poor Phil Kingcup being lost. I was coming back from Cherbourg the same night; werry stormy it was, though I've seen wuss, still there was the douce of a kick-up of sea.

"We was going to start together, but when we got under weigh Phil sung out they wouldn't be ready for another half-hour - had

to get their to'sl down and stowed. But, after a bit, we see'd em following, and that was the last was ever seen of the boat under sail.

"Next that was heard of her was when she drifted on shore, with all her tubs hung round her, and the ballast gone, by Hope Cove. The bodies - four of 'em - was seen lying on the bottom, in deep water, just outside. I saw them mysel; t'was the strangest sight I ever see'd, for you could tell their faces as they laid on the bottom, it was that clear."

Foot note: If you stand in Hope Cove near the lifeboat house and look out over the wall towards the harbour on your right, the last rock linked by a wall to form the harbour arm is called "Brandy Rock". Though this may refer to a wreck, it is more likely a reminder of the days when smugglers "sowed their crop" by this rock.

You'll see from the report of the death of Kingcup and his crew that when his boat came ashore she had "all her tubs hung around her". This is the way the smugglers often avoided the Customs men and still got their goods ashore. Instead of landing the tubs of brandy straight on to a beach and risking running into the arms and swords of the Riding Officers, the tubs were slung over the sides of the boat on ropes, rigged with kegs, then a weight (usually a stone with a hole drilled in it), then more kegs and then a stone and so on.

The boat with the kegs slung like this would come as close as she dared in the dark to some prominent landmark and cut free the lashing. The kegs would then pull the stones off the deck, sink to the seabed and be held in place by the stone anchors. Later it was up to the locals to gather in "the crop". Their crabbing work was a fine excuse to be hauling up lines to objects on the bottom. To collect the tubs, the crabber would "creep" the bottom with a grapnel and hook the lines linking the tubs together. Brandy Rock was probably one of the places for sowing the crop. After that the tubs would be carried to a safe hiding place.

In Bantham, smuggled tubs were hidden in a loft hidey-hole, via a trap-door right over the two forges in Whiddon's blacksmith shop. The little windows under the thatched roofs of Bantham cottages are known as "smugglers eyes". A house, The Whiddons, now stands on the site of the smithy at the seaward end of the village just before the gate to Bantham Ham.

In Thurlestone they stowed the tubs on the roof of the church porch. One Thurlestone man who died in 1900 at the age of 91, told his Rector: "Many and many a time I carried up a ladder as many as fifty barrels of spirits on a dark night and hid them on the top of the roof of the church porch

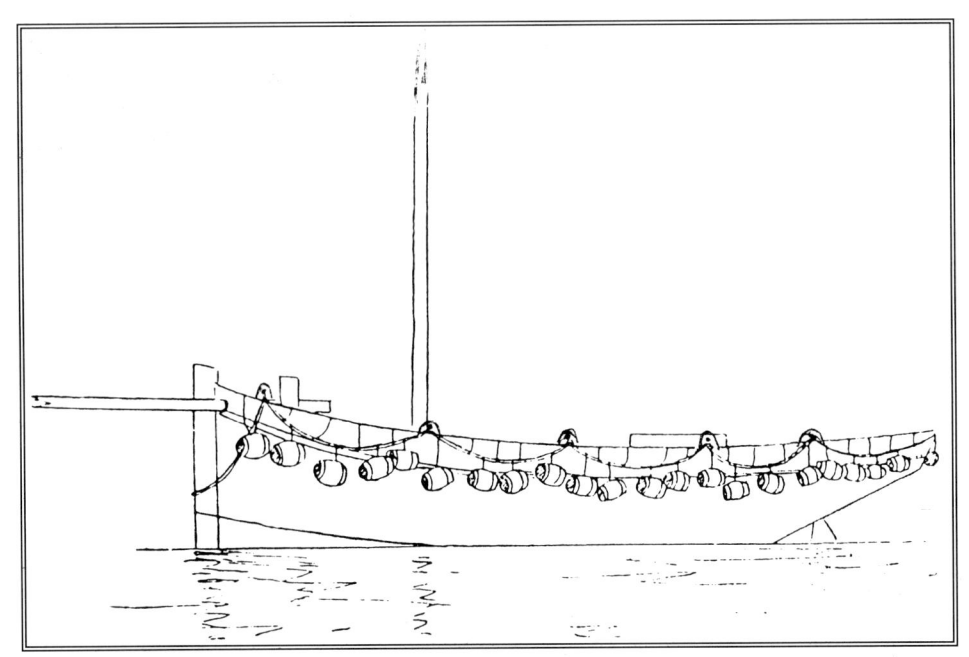

This is how Phil Kingcup's Boat would have been rigged for "sowing the crop".

behind the battlements. Us always kept the tower door locked them times, lest one should go up and look down over".

In Hope they went up under the thatch of the old village, now known as Inner Hope. Sometimes they were thatched right in so that even a search of the loft space would find nothing.

21. HMS RAMILLIES.
Ramillies Hole, 1760.

THIS was one of the greatest tragedies in the records of the Royal Navy, 708 men and a child died when the 90-gun warship *Ramillies* smashed into the 300 foot high cliffs near Bolt Tail on February 15, 1760. Only 26 men survived and many of them were so badly injured that they never served the Navy again.

The loss was a great national disaster. The news shocked the whole country though the naval towns were hardest hit by the huge loss of life. In Portsmouth, for example, the local newspaper reported: "Words cannot describe the consternation of the people of the town. Nothing but weeping and wailing is heard in every street...wives for their husbands, parents for their children, and children for their fathers. Others lament the loss of friends..."

The hurricane that was the cause of it all struck Southern England on February 14. Trees were torn up, houses disintegrated, haystacks disappeared. In London a pinnacle of a building adjoining the House of Commons crashed through the roof of Parliament, narrowly missing the Speaker's chair. The lead on the Admiralty roof rolled up like a scroll.

The Mall was blocked by fallen trees and branches. Great thunderclaps, lightning flashes, hail and sleet added to the damage as the great storm roared on. In every harbour in the South, ships were smashed and sailors drowned. At sea, conditions were so appalling that ships ran before it with bare poles and struggled desperately to find some sort of shelter from the stormy blasts.

Ramillies was out there and in desperate trouble. She was amongst giant breaking seas in mid-Channel somewhere off the Brittany peninsula. She had sailed from Plymouth on February 6 with the rest of the Channel Squadron under the command of Admiral Edward Boscawen. His orders were to join the rest of the Fleet in Quiberon Bay and Boscawen was more than impatient to get there. His two previous attempts to do so had failed due to the weather and strong westerlies and so, despite winds that were distinctly unfavourable, he had sailed again. He was in his flagship, the *Royal William,* a first rate of 100 guns. In addition to *Ramillies*, his squadron consisted of the 98-gun *Sandwich, St.George* of 96 guns, *Pricess Amelia* with 80 cannon, the 36-gun frigate *Venus* and a 10-gun sloop called *Hawk.*

Together the squadron fought their way down Channel. By the 12th the southwesterly was freshening. Squalls of rain and sleet made altering sail a misery for all aboard. Then came the fore-runners of the hurricane - gales tore at them and swung from south-west to north-west and back again. "The gales were so violent," wrote Admiral Boscawen later, "that I could seldom carry a topsail". On the night of February 13 it became so bad they were obliged to lie-to with bare masts. On the 14th the real hurricane reached them. *Royal William* had all her sails split, was repeatedly pooped by huge seas and suffered severe damage to parts of her decking.

It says a lot for the seamanship of *Ramillies'* captain, who bore the strange name of Wittewronge Taylor that up to that point *Ramillies* had stayed with the flagship. *Ramillies* was long past her prime and was once again leaking badly. Some parts of her were nearly 100 years old. She had been launched first in 1664 as the *Katherine*. She was rebuilt in 1702 and became the *Royal Katherine* and then rebuilt again in 1749 from which work she emerged as *Ramillies*. And she leaked no matter what her name.

In fact, she leaked so badly that Admiral Hawke had to move his flag from her to the *Royal George* only days before his great victory at Quiberon Bay on November 20, 1759 and left Wittewronge Taylor, his flag-captain, to sail her

Kendall McDonald examines one of the great cannon underwater in Ramillies Hole, a sea cave which runs right under the coastal path.

back to Plymouth for repairs. So Captain Taylor missed that battle and was lumbered with the leaky old Ramillies until he died with her. Wittewrong Taylor got his name as a descendant of a Dutch family which had settled in Britain before the time of the Spanish Armada. He first reached captain rank when he was given command of *Magnamine* in 1755. The next year he obviously thought he now had enough naval pay to take a wife and he married Catherine

Vincent of Stoke Damerel, Devonport at Exeter on September 28,1756. He then served in the *Malborough* and the *Royal William*.

The repairs to *Ramillies* had taken until the New Year of 1760 when she was ordered to rejoin the Channel Squadron under its new commander in succession to Hawke, Admiral Edward Boscawen. The Honorable Edward Boscawen was a fine seamen, a stern, but not unfriendly man, an odd mixture of sea-dog and scholar, who could write letters to his wife before setting off on some long voyage which contained such poetic sentiments as "To be sure I lose the fruits of the earth, but then I am gathering the flowers of the sea".

The repairs to *Ramillies* at Plymouth Dockyard could hardly have been well done. The leaks in her were now so severe that all hands were at the pumps and teams of men with buckets were bailing too. One of her timbers seemed to have given and she was making water so fast that Captain Taylor ordered the shot taken out of some of the guns and lights made ready so that they could fire the guns and hoist the lights to signal their distress. It was now the evening of February 14.

The reason that those distress signals were not made tells us a great deal about the discipline of the Navy at that time. It may also tell us something of the regard which Edward Boscawen was held in by his fellow officers. For there seems to have been some sort of conference on board *Ramillies* between the captain, the senior officers and the ship's sailing master. Their decision was that it would be better to bear away without making the signal of distress "as some other of the squadron might take it to be the Admiral". Clearly that would never do!

So Ramillies, despite the water slopping about in her guts and despite the desperate pumping and bailing necessary to keep her afloat, hoisted a foresail and drew away from the flagship into the dark. All that night she ran for Plymouth, up Channel with the hurricane behind her. When the dawn came her crew could see nothing more than in the night. Until at about ten in the morning there came a lull in the wind and as the spray dropped, one of the midshipmen shouted "Land-ho!", but by the time all eyes on deck had followed his pointing finger, the gap was gone although one or two officers confirmed that there had been something that looked vaguely like land on their port bow. Anything was better than nothing and the Sailing Master of *Ramillies* ordered the mainsail set and headed the ship to the north-east.

The Master had not seen the land himself and after half an hour on their new course without any further sighting, he doubted if anyone else had. But suddenly, clear for all to see was the undoubted shape of an island and behind it the main shore.

The Master identified the island as Looe Island, which meant they were still to the west of Plymouth and the shelter of the Sound was not far away. He had made a terrible mistake. He had got the wrong island. What he had seen was in fact Burgh Island at the entrance to the Avon at Bantham. He was 26 miles further to the east than he thought. Worse still he was well within the great sweep of Bigbury Bay, so far in that he could see that Burgh Island was an island and you have to be really close to the shore to see that when approaching from the west.

Ramillies was now on a lee shore with a giant south-westerly blowing her to disaster. The only thing to do was to stay in Bigbury Bay, perhaps by anchoring until the wind dropped. But the Sailing Master made yet another terrible decision. He decided to try and round what he thought was Rame Head and get into the shelter of Plymouth Sound. But it wasn't Rame Head, it was Bolt Tail and there was no shelter the other side of it, just five miles of towering cliffs.

It is important to know here that the sailing master in those days was exactly that - he was in command of the actual sailing of the ship. Though he was under the direction of the captain, many sailing decision were taken by him on his own authority. This decision to round what he thought was Rame Head was his, though it seems the Captain and some other officers disagreed with him. But not apparently strongly enough.

By now the ship had been seen from the land. Looking down on her from the heights of Bolt Tail were most of the population of Hope who had struggled up against the howling wind. So valuable to the ordinary people was a wreck that as many as ten thousand people have been recorded gathering when a ship was seen to be trapped in the bay. And as the ship moved back and forth, attempting to claw her way out to the open sea, so the crowds would move along the coast keeping pace with her. This time the watchers on the shore would have been disappointed that she was a warship. Navy ships provided poor pickings when compared with a merchantman driven ashore.

But whatever kind of ship she was, those watching were surprised to see her set all sails including her topsails and attempt to run to the eastward. The Sailing Master realised his mistake too late. Too late he changed his mind and attempted to stay the ship, but the wind carried her on. So strong was that wind that it used her masts and free-flailing sails to push her on.

At this moment Captain Wittewronge Taylor seems to have snatched back command of his ship from the Sailing Master. "Let go the mainsheet," he shouted and two sailors, William Wise and Robuck, did as they were ordered. But it was too late again.

The amount of water in her made her almost uncontrollable. Either the mainmast fell or was cut away to reduce windage, the mizzenmast followed it. Now those villagers on Bolt Tail were looking almost directly down on *Ramillies*. She was only 400 yards from the rocks. The main anchor was ordered down, but when it stuck, the smaller bow anchor was cut free and both anchors fell together. Both cables raced out, but crossed one another. Even so they brought the ship bow to wind and held her there. There was no hope of sailing the ship out of her fix and so the foremast was cut down. As it went it took the bowsprit with it. It was now two o'clock in the afternoon.

The wind didn't slacken. In fact it started increasing. "I think from the hour of two in the afternoon, it blew stronger that I ever felt it in my life," wrote Admiral Boscawen in his log. That wind blew the *St. George* and the *Venus* all the way back to Spithead. The *Hawk* simply disappeared forever with all hands.

The anchors held *Ramillies* until just before dusk, when the two anchor cables, sawing violently across each other at the jerk of each and every wave, finally parted. The next giant swell swung her broadside to the cliff. Down went her sheet anchor, but before they could give it enough cable to hold, her starboard side struck the rocks. Her bow ground round and she was in a great crushing machine between walls of water and the cliffs.

White water foamed over her. The Captain of Marines went off his head and marched up and down the poop singing and declaiming poetry. The Boatswain had brought his young son to sea with him and now tried to save the child by flinging him up on to the rocks, only to see the child land on his head and dash his brains out. Seconds later the bosun's lifeless body joined that of his son in the surf.

Captain Wittewronge Taylor and the other officers waited as long as they dared and then jumped from the poop. They all fell short and were carried away in the foam.

The men struggled to get on the starboard rails or upper gun-ports to jump for the shore. The sensible timed their jump between waves, but it didn't help. Most went to their deaths like straws as the sea flung them high up the cliff face. Only 26 managed to get some sort of grip and drag themselves into cracks in the rocks where the waves could not reach them.

William Wise was the last man to get away. He let down the starboard stern ladder, scrambled down the ropes and threw him on to the rocks. A wave lifted the stern of the ship and dropped part of it down on his right leg, turning it into a bloody bruise. Despite this, he got up and hopped and dragged himself up a small gully. When he looked back the ship had gone. All that was left looked like firewood and that and the mangled bodies of his shipmates were pounding against the cliff face or being flung in and out of a cave which opened just where the ship had struck.

William Wise pulled himself tuft by tuft of grass up the gully until he reached a deep hole close to the top. He fell into this pit and passed out. When he came too, it was the dark before dawn.

The news of the loss of *Ramillies* and over 700 men shocked the nation and the Navy. It shocked Admiral Boscawen who first heard of it when he finally got *Royal William* back into Plymouth in the afternoon of February 16, where he found both *Princess Amelia* and *Sandwich* "much shattered". His report of the loss to the Admiralty relies much on the account of William Wise, who was found in that pit on the cliffs and carried down to Hope the next day. That letter can be seen today in the Public Record Office at Kew. It reads:

"On Thursday 14th instant in the close of the evening the Ramillies being in company with the Admiral, observed the Admiral to lower his main topsail, but could not see whether it was taken in. However, Captain Taylor ordered his to be lowered and as soon as it was dark, furled it. The ship then making much water, having sprung a leak under the larboard entering port, William Wise imagined a butt to have started near the place.

"As soon as the main topsail was handed, Capt.Taylor ordered guns to be unshotted and signal lights to be got ready for making the signal of Distress;- but on consultation, concluded it would be better to bear away without making the signal of distress as some other of the squadron might take it to be the Admiral. They were now employed at all the pumps and buckets and hawled the main sail up and bore away under a foresail.

"About ten or eleven in the morning steering about E.by N, some of the officers thought they saw the land, but the weather was so extream thick that few believed it to be the land. The master not convinced it was the land stood in to make it; got their larboard Fore-tack to the cat head and set the mainsail; about eleven they saw the land, and the master seeing Burrow Island which lays in Bigberry Bay took it for the Loo Island, and concluded they were to the westward of Plymouth.

"About this time the people on shore saw the ship, and as they say, she was rather to the northward of the Bolt, and were in hopes that she would have brought up in Bigberry Bay rather than attempt to weather the Bolt, as a very great swell set right on it; but to their surprize they saw her wear, and get their starboard tacks on board and set their topsails.

"They now endeavoured to weather the Easternmost Point, taking it for the Ramhead; set the courses and close reef'd topsails: The Captain, as well as some other Officers, said they could not weather the land; the Master was persuaded they could, but soon saw his mistake, and endeavoured to stay the ship and get into Bigberry Bay; but the great swell, together with her having much water in her hold would not admit of it.

"At this time Wm.Wise and Robuck were standing by the Main sheet; they heard somebody say the mainmast is sprung; and presently they heard the Captain call, "Let go the Mainsheet". Which they did and ran directly upon deck, where they found the Main mast gone and presently the Mizon mast. - Wise then heard the Master call, "Let go the anchor and clew up forward," which was done; they then let go another anchor and cut away their foremast, which carried the Bowsprit with it; this was about two o'clock, and the ship abour a quarter of a mile from the Bolt's Tail, but the weather was so thick that as yet they did not know the land. She rode till the dusk of the evening when she drove; they then let go the sheet anchor, but before they could give her cable to bring up, she struck with her starboard quarter, and her bow then drove to the westward and took the rocks.

"William Wise who seems to be clear in his account, says that he was the last man that jumped on shore; he let loose the starboard stern ladder, and went down it, and threw himself on the rocks where the ship fell on his right leg and bruised it to pieces, but that he got up in that condition and looked back, and could not see any more of the ship. - The stem is drove into a cave to the eastward, where she struck and most of the men lay in the surf of that cave; but the ship drove to such small pieces that it appears like piles of firewood. - One of her cables lays over a rock and seems to have hold of the bow of her, but it is impossible to be certain where her bottom lays untill fine weather admits of boats making a stricter survey."

E.Boscawen.

Also in the Public Record Office at Kew is this one to the Admiral from his special envoy, Benjamin Hall, one of the Master Attendants of Plymouth Dockyard, whom Boscawen sent to the wreck scene to see what could be salvaged:

Thurlestone,
Feb.17 - 1760

Honourable Sir,
At one this afternoon I gott to the place where the ship was lost which is a litel to the Eastward of the Bolt Head in the dismal spot that fate designed her - She is intireley under water and what comes from her no boat can ventur to save yet as the sea is very high but as the wind is at N.W. hope tomorrow at low water to take up all the Ironwork and gather things that comes on shore and give it to the care of the officers of the Customs. I cant see aney part of her, mast sails or yards soe I think the sea has split and torn them to pieces without they lay in coves that I cant see without a boat - this evening I went to the village where some of the seamen was that was saved and told them the Admirals orders they that are able gave me there word of coming to Dartm. tomorrow and those that are lame ask me how there landlords is to be paid to that I can give no answer - Sir I hope what I shale doe tomorrow will meet with your aprobation to sound in her as the guns is falling in her hole and the Fishermen told me at low water its three fathom. I shale take wot step I can to preserve all the stores I can and waite your Honble Command.
I am, Sir, your most obedient Humble servant to command
BENJ. HALL

It is interesting to note that even Benjamin Hall got muddled over where he was - in this letter calling Bolt Tail, Bolt Head!

It seems from an investigation by divers of the wreck site over several years recently that Benjamin Hall must have mounted a major seaborne salvage operation as most of the "Ironwork", that is cannon, are no longer there. Some evidence of this salvage being made by boat comes from a discovery by other divers of one of the biggest cannon of *Ramillies* - a 32-pounder, nine feet six inches long and weighing nearly three tons - lying on the sandy seabed just to the west of the disturbed water you can see forming a small race or riptide off Bolt Tail. This lone gun was probably the result of an accident when the cannon, slung

The start of Benjamin Hall's letter

Children digging on Thurlestone Sands in 1963 uncovered nine skeletons in a mass grave - probably sailors from the Ramillies. Picture shows Kingsbridge Police Constable Ernie Tucker clearing sand away from some of the bones.

beween lifting barges, were being taken into Hope Cove.

Much less care was taken with the bodies of the crew which were washed up on the beaches for miles around. They were stripped of anything useable and buried in holes dug in the sand. In recent years some of their skeletons have been uncovered by enthusiastic sandcastle builders, much to the consternation of the diggers' parents! Unidentified bodies washed ashore were always buried in unmarked graves dug into the beach or sandhills nearby until an Act of Parliament in July 1808 required all bodies cast ashore to be buried in a churchyard's consecrated ground.

Among items discovered by divers on the wreck site and now to be seen at the Shipwreck Centre, at Charlestown, Cornwall, are seamen's rings, usually given to them by their sweethearts. Two from the *Ramillies* say: "I like my choice" and "When money is low it must go".

Foot Note: The wreck of the *Ramillies* is **not** in Ramillies Cove which you will see marked on Ordnance Survey maps and never has been, but is two coves to the east at Whitechurch, where "Ramillies Hole" is the eastern of two caves on either side of a large jutting rock. Once on the cliff path here don't try peering over the edge - grass is slippery stuff; wet grass is like ice - as you won't be able to see into the caves. But you are standing on the spot where all those watchers saw the end of *Ramillies* and on the spot where Benjamin Hall discovered that she had been smashed to pieces. Beneath your feet way down in the cave are two of her giant cannon which escaped his salvage work. And just to complete the story - one of those holes near the path was known for at least a century after the wreck as "William Wise's Pit", but today no one seems to know which it was. Take your pick of the pits!

The Jebba shortly after dawn on March 18, 1907. The rocket apparatus ropes are still attached to the ship.

22. JEBBA.
Graystone Ledge, 1907.

THE seas were already more than rough when the *Jebba* entered the Channel on the Sunday night of March 17, 1907.

What made matters worse was that the high seas were accompanied by thick fog despite the strong winds from the south-west - a strange combination, but not a rare one as far as the Channel is concerned.

Captain J.J.C. Mills was a Plymouth man and had met the mix before. This didn't mean that he wasn't a worried man as he stood on the bridge that night. He was heading for

Plymouth, where he intended to land 30 passengers and some of the 100 bags of Royal Mail, which he was carrying from south-west and west coasts of Africa. His final destination, however, was Liverpool, the home port of the *Jebba*.

Captain Mills was worried more about the fog than the waves. The fog was the reason for the *Jebba*'s engines being at dead slow rather than the comfort of his 79 passengers, who included 20 women and several invalids, who had succumbed to the various tolls that colonial service in Africa had extracted from their health. The truth was that Captain Mills was worried too, because none of his lookouts had sighted the Eddystone Light and he knew, that fog or no fog, they should have caught a glimmer of it by now.

The *Jebba* had originally been named the *Albertville* when she was built by Sir Raylton Dixon and Company in Middlesbrough in 1896. She was a steel vessel of 3813 tons, 352ft long with a 44ft beam. When she was bought by the Elder Dempster Line her name was changed to *Jebba*.

On this voyage her holds were packed with goods from West Africa - palm oil, rubber, ivory, palm kernels, cocoa, tomatoes and fruit of many kinds. There was also one box of coins. Most of her passengers were Government officials, mining men and traders. There were 76 crew aboard, many of whom were Kroos, West African negroes from Liberia, famous for their skill as seamen.

The crew had instructions that nothing was too good for their passengers. For example, in anticipation of their arrival at Plymouth, the 30 passengers who were to leave the ship there were invited to a special supper - in case the earlier eight-course dinner had not been enough for them!

The bell for this celebration supper sounded at one o'clock in the morning of Monday, March 18, 1907. As they pulled out their chairs to sit down, there was a harsh grinding sound and a slight shock.

The noise and the shock were, in fact, the result of the *Jebba* running hard aground. Some of the other passengers and crew hurried on deck, one or two in their nightclothes. There was no panic and if there was the slightest sign of one, it was soon dispelled by the immediate response to the ship's distress rockets. A flare appeared high on the cliffs above them to show that they had been seen.

That flare had been ignited by one of the Hope Cove Coastguards, Edward Reed, who was in the lookout post, which today is close to the footpath, but is unmanned. The quick appearance of that answering flare and the cool, calm attitude of the crew soon convinced the passengers that hitting the rocks was only a temporary nuisance, and those planning to get off at Plymouth were so convinced that they would be landed there within an hour or two that they sat down again and got on with their special supper. When they finished, coffee and biscuits were handed round with a glass or two of something warming, and the chief steward's report says "everything was then done to take the passengers' minds off what had occurred". Quite what that was, apart from more rounds of brandies and liqueurs, it is hard to guess. But when water started filling the ship's holds, the crew's attitude changed very swiftly.

In fact, Captain Mills gave the order to launch a boat and then countermanded the order when the seas started breaking right over his ship.

On shore, Edward Reed had now alerted the Coastguard Station down in Hope Cove and the rescue teams swung into action. First to go was the Hope Cove lifeboat, the fourth at that station to bear the name *Alexandra*. This one was beamier than the earlier boats, 35 feet long and fitted for twelve oars. In command when she was launched was Coxswain James Edward Thornton. The huge waves made the launch difficult and villagers stood up to their waists among the great swells to get the lifeboat clear of the beach. At 2.15 a.m. the lifeboat reached the ship. She was now broadside on to the cliffs just inside the Greystone Ledge and about 100 feet out from cliff face. Her starboard rail was under water and heavy seas were breaking over her decks

Cox'n Thornton sized up the situation at once. As there were rocks under both bow and stern there was no chance of the lifeboat running inside her to sheltered water. To take people off from the side towards the open sea would have meant dragging each one of the 155 aboard in a breeches buoy through the huge seas battering the ship's sides. Several would be bound to die in such an operation. Thornton knew that the rocket apparatus was on its way, so he and his crew stood off and waited to make sure they were at hand if needed later.

On land, the problem was to get the rocket apparatus into position above the wreck. However, with the help of teams of horses and the man-power of most of the villagers of Hope, the equipment was pulled up Bolt Tail and along the cliff top to the scene of the wreck.

The first rocket was a good shot, but the line slipped down her forestay into the sea. The second rocket curved right over her amidships and was quickly made fast by members of the crew.

It was a hell of a haul up to the top of the cliffs from the ship 200 feet below, but the coastguards started work. A little girl was the first to come up; then a woman passenger; then a woman stewardess. It was clearly a very risky route to safety and the gusts of wind made it even more dangerous. While the coastguards carried out these rescues and began to wonder about continuing, two local fishermen, Isaac Jarvis and Jack Argeat, volunteered to climb down the cliff and try and set up other lines to the ship lower down. Somehow in the wind and the dark, the two men found a better place to bring people ashore - and it was almost level with the ship. The men quickly set up two more bosun's chairs and the passengers were soon coming ashore quickly along this shorter and safer route. In fact, only 38 people were saved by the long route to the top of the cliffs. The other 117 got ashore by the fishermen's lines. Captain Mills was the last to leave his ship.

Isaac Jarvis and Jack Argeat were later awarded the Albert Medal for their bravery and their medals were presented by King Edward VII(See Wreck No 63). It was said locally that the two men were great grandsons of Hope villagers who had helped the few survivors up those same cliffs from the wreck of *HMS Ramillies* a few yards further west in 1760!

Thousands of people came to see the *Jebba* (as they had nearly 150 years before to see the close-by wreckage of *Ramillies*). They came from miles about and the path along the cliffs from Hope Cove was turned into an earth road by their feet.

Looking down on her from above she was completely broadside to the cliff with her bows to the east. From the moment she was wrecked she was pounded by big seas. When things were more settled, all the mail bags were saved and most of the passengers' baggage. The box of coins was quickly taken ashore. A small ship managed to get alongside during a period of calm and took off most of the deck cargo of tomatoes. Helmet divers managed to get down at the same time and they confirmed the obvious -

By May, her back was broken, her funnel had gone and her holds were broken open.

the Jebba was now full of water and so badly damaged that there was no chance of saving her because of the big gashes in her hull. Most of her cargo was saved, however. All the rubber was brought off, and nearly all of the ivory, though some tusks were reported missing. Divers set to work to salvage her bronze propellor, but had to blow it apart with explosives and then raise it blade by blade. Each blade was then worth about £250.

The fruit in her holds soon began to work out of holes in her hull and littered beaches for miles down the coast. By May 3, six weeks after her wrecking, she had sunk down and her back was broken. She now had a much heavier list to seaward and though her masts still stood, her funnel had disappeared. By full summer there was nothing to be seen of her.

Foot Note: At very low spring tides the top of one of her four boilers can just be seen to break water. Animal lovers will like to know that the ship's cat, two chimpanzees and many parrots, the crew's pets, were saved soon after the wreck. The parrots were given to local people. If you find a pub in the area with a parrot, you may be sure you will be told that it came from the *Jebba*!

23. BLESK.
The Gray Stone, 1896

TODAY it is a sad fact of life that if you walk on a British beach you may well get oil or tar on your feet. But there was a time when such sticky things were completely unknown. There was a time when the idea of a shipwreck polluting miles and miles of beaches just never crossed anyone's mind.

That happy time came to an end on December 1, 1896, when, in lashing rain and gale-force winds, the first wreck of an oil tanker in the world brought large-scale pollution to the coast of the South Hams. It was a warning of things to come, but no one, of course, could imagine such a future...

Victoria the First, Queen of the United Kingdom, Empress of India, had five more glorious years to reign when the Russian steamer called *Blesk* left the Black Sea port of Batum on November 14, 1896, and headed through the Mediterranean towards her final destination of Hamburg.

The *Blesk*, built in 1890, was one of the first ships in the world specially designed to carry a full cargo of petroleum. The very first was the *Gluckauf*, built in Britain in 1886. But she and the *Blesk* were never described as "tankers". To the Victorians they were still "steamships" even if they did have their engine rooms at the stern and all forward of that were special tanks for the oil.

Carrying a full load of 3,180 tons of petrol-oil, the Blesk's 265 h.p. engines could push her 298 feet through the sea at a cruising speed of 10 knots. In pictures of the time she looks a little like a modern tanker because of her single funnel near the stern. On this last voyage she called at Constantinople and then again at Gibraltar for coal. On November 28, 1896, while in sight of Cape Finisterre, she ran into a storm. That was her last sight of land until she was wrecked four days later.

On December 1, out in the Channel, she did, however, see a light. Captain Adolph Deme assumed it was the Corbier lighthouse and altered his course more to the north. That the light was the Eddystone never crossed his mind. The *Blesk* was now on collision course with the Bolt.

As she steamed across Bigbury Bay at 8.50 p.m., the keeper of the watch at Prawle Point coastguard station noted that the barometer was falling fast. He also logged the outside temperature as 46 degrees F.

At sea, Captain Deme was surprised to see the lights of a big steamer, which steadily overhauled him on a parallel course. It was a comforting sight as the visibility ahead of him seemed to be nil. The *Blesk* altered course slightly and settled down in the steamer's wake.

At Prawle, they wrote in the log under the weather heading: "Thick with rain". As far as Captain Deme was concerned that would be an understatement. He could see nothing, but confident that he was following a big steamer, he kept his speed at a steady ten knots.

He was still doing ten knots at 9.08 p.m. precisely when the *Blesk* ran into and up on the Gray Stone, a great rock a little to the east of Bolt Tail. When Captain Deme got back to his feet, he swung his engine room telegraph to the Russian equivalent of "Full speed astern". The propellor churned away, but his ship was on too hard to come off. Captain Deme's next orders were for distress rockets to be fired and for the boats to be swung out. His rockets were

The Blesk had rammed the Gray Stone at full speed.

seen despite the weather because he was very close to a Coastguard lookout.

Both the Hope Cove and the Salcombe lifeboats were launched and, being the closest, the Hope Cove lifeboat, *Alexandra*, a new self-righting boat of 34 feet, fitted for ten oars, was first on the scene. She made two trips to the wreck taking off all the 43 men aboard and landing them safely in Hope. The rocket apparatus was manhandled along to the site of the wreck, but arrived too late to be of help.

The lifeboat men were sure she was finished from the moment that they saw her. She was, of course, badly holed forward, but the crew said the engine room and stern area were still free of water. However, anyone looking down from the cliffs on the foggy dawn of December 2, would have seen little chance of salvage. Huge seas were pounding the wreck and she was moving slightly at each blow. At 10.18 a.m. Hope Cove coastguards reported that she was now broadside on. It was then that the first glistening streaks in the hollows behind the breaking billows showed that her oil tanks were ruptured. The pollution had begun.

Just after midday two tugs from Plymouth, the *Vixen* and the *Belle* could be seen as the fog started to lift, but when they could not get near because of the huge seas, they gave up and steamed away. Some of the *Blesk*'s crew asked to be put back aboard by the lifeboat. But the swell over the Gray Stone made the lifeboat cox'n refuse to risk it.

Now the oil could be seen quite clearly. A great band of smoother water lay off the coast for nearly 400 yards out to sea. Crowds of watchers lined the cliffs above the wreck. Soon the first dead bass floated belly up into Salcombe Estuary. Many other dead fish followed. It was only a foretaste of what was to come. First the fish, then the oiled seabirds, dying in the black line which marked high tide on the beaches and rocks. They could smell her cargo in Kingsbridge and some said in Totnes too, 20 miles away. Many shell fishermen had poor catches and their pot lines oozed oil for months afterwards.

However upsetting this was for the locals, they didn't take it out on the crew, who stayed at the Hope and Anchor Inn in Hope Cove and were well looked after. Provisions for the sailors were sent by the Shipwrecked Mariners' Society branch at Salcombe. The acting Russian consul, a Mr.Bellamy of Plymouth, soon arrived on the scene and had the crew moved from Hope to Salcombe and then to Kingsbridge to catch the London train.

At high water, the sea increased. Rivets could be heard snapping like rifle shots, and the waves striking the now-empty tanks boomed like distant big guns. The seas starting breaking right over her and, as the funnel toppled overboard, the ship parted in the middle. At 4.45 p.m the Lloyds' agent, looking down from the cliffs, saw both halves underwater. Later he cabled Lloyds "Total loss"

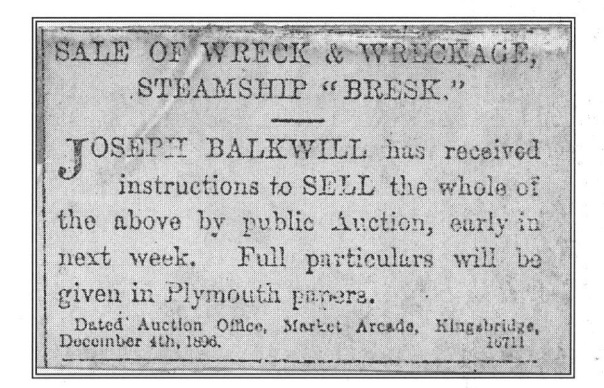

> SALE OF WRECK & WRECKAGE,
> STEAMSHIP "BRESK."
>
> JOSEPH BALKWILL has received instructions to SELL the whole of the above by public Auction, early in next week. Full particulars will be given in Plymouth papers.
>
> Dated Auction Office, Market Arcade, Kingsbridge, December 4th, 1896.   16711

On Tuesday, December 8, just a week after she tried to climb up on to the land, the wreck "together with any cargo that might remain" was sold by Kingsbridge auctioneer, Mr.Joseph Balkwill, at Hope Cove. At that public auction she fetched £375.

Foot Note: The wreck today is completely shattered and her parts lie both sides of the Gray Stone. The Gray Stone is easy to see from the path - it is exactly that, a grey stone and a big one at that.

24. JANE ROWE
Bolberry Down, 1914

THOUGH always smartly turned-out, this lady was a tramp. That is she "tramped" the world's oceans in search of work. She was launched as the *Mary Thomas* in 1889, but her name was later changed to *Barto*. Her name had changed again to *Jane Rowe* when this 1259-ton Swedish steamer, whose home port was Gefle, set out from Cardiff with a cargo of coal on January 27, 1914, and delivered this to Oran on February 4. She was in Oran for a fortnight, then sailed for Rotterdam on February 18, her holds crammed with 3,000 tons of iron ore.

It was to be her last voyage. In dense fog on February 28, she went ashore at exactly 10.29am and sat on an even keel on a sandbank among rocks under Bolberry Down, three-quarters of a mile to the west of Lantern Rock. She looked as though she would float off easily when first spotted by the pleasure steamer *Kingsbridge Packet* on her regular early-

Tugs tried to pull the Jane Rowe free.

morning run from Salcombe to Plymouth. The *Kingsbridge Packet* got a hawser across, but no amount of pulling would shift her. By the next day there were five local tugs, *Dragon*, *Totnes*, *Boarhound*, *Dencaba* and *Venture*, all pulling at her without success. Then it was too late. At 10.30am on March 1 all the crew of 21 were taken off by breeches buoy as the *Jane Rowe* was pushed further in onto the rocks by the rising tide. Soon she was broadside on, with the seas breaking over her. Within a short time all four of her holds and the engine room were pierced. She was soon a total wreck. A good mark for the totally broken wreckage is the boiler of the Lowestoft steam-drifter Charter, which came ashore close by in 1933 (see Wreck No.25)

The Jane Rowe ashore under Bolberry Down. Note the Salcombe lifeboat near the bow.

Foot Note: The danger of getting too close to the edge of the cliff is obvious, but not always kept sufficiently in mind - a 15-year-old boy and his employer both fell over the cliffs here when they joined the huge crowd watching the various attempts to get the *Jane Rowe* free! They were both lucky to survive.

25. CHARTER.
Ralph's Hole, 1933.

A LOWESTOFT wooden steam drifter of 96 tons, *Charter* was wrecked on January 7, 1933, when fishing out of Plymouth. She went ashore in the afternoon near Ralph's Hole, a cave at the far western end of Cathole Cliff.

She was undamaged, despite a fresh wind and ground swell, until the tide went out, then she fell over on to her side. Despite the efforts of the ten-man crew, who tried to save her on the next tide, she was found to be too badly damaged to sail again. She is now in very small pieces Her boiler shows at most stages of the tide except full high.

The date of her wrecking was exactly one year after she had been forced to put back into Plymouth with two other steam drifters, after running into a massive westerly gale. Three of the crew had to be taken to hospital with head injuries. In that incident the Charter had lost all her nets, having to cut them away.

26. DRAGON.
Cathole Cliff, 1757

CHILDREN on their way home to school died when this West Indiaman smashed into the towering walls of Cathole Cliffs on August 23, 1757. The *Dragon* was driven in by a south-westerly gale.

The brig was homeward-bound from Jamaica to London with a cargo of rum and sugar, one of the many ships taking part in the boom in trade with the West Indies.

In the wreck it seems to be the passengers who suffered most. In Malborough Churchyard, for example, there is a tombstone which reads: "Here lye the bodies of Rhodes-Daniel, Mary, and Joseph Chambers, sons and daughter of Edward Chambers of Jamaica, who were shipwrecked at Cat-hole within this parish". Nine people were drowned, but the captain and ten crew were saved. The children of settlers were often sent back "home" to Britain to go to school, and this seems the likely reason for the Chambers children being aboard.

After an eight-year search local diver Bill Bunting believes he has found her wreckage, including cannon and shot. The wreck is close in near Lantern Rock.

The Charter became a total wreck. Her boiler shows at most states of the tide.

27. WESTMORELAND.
West of the Ham Stone, 1871

THE coconuts, packed between the casks of rum to stop them shifting in rough seas, were washed ashore in every cove for miles around. The sugar in her cargo melted in the water. And those casks of rum which were washed ashore were smashed by the coastguards to stop anyone killing themselves by drinking the overproof spirit.

The 132-foot-long *Westmoreland*, a lively barque of 450 tons, had made a fast passage from Jamaica and Captain Thomas Gaskin and his crew of 14, plus their single passenger, a 14-year-old boy, had high hopes of being in London in record time. That was until they ran into fog at the entrance to the Channel. They reduced sail and the lookouts strained to see the Start Light. Just before midnight on Thursday, July 13, 1871, the fog suddenly lifted and the shore seemed less that a mile away. Captain Gaskin tried to put about, but she failed to come round, probably because there was too little sail on her, and drove on to some rocks under the steep cliffs surrounding the next bay to the west of Soar Mill Cove.

Directly she struck the seas started to break over her and she swung broadside on to the cliffs, then started to list into the waves on to her starboard side. The pinnace and dinghy were launched and all aboard got into them without mishap. The crew wanted to make straight for the land, but Captain Gaskin, seeing the tall band of surf at the foot of the cliffs, ordered them to wait in the tolerably smooth water in lee of the ship until daybreak.

At dawn it was clear how wise he had been. The barque lay in the middle of the little bay which has a curve of about half a mile. The whole of this area was covered with large loose rocks, many tons in weight, and at high water mark the cliffs zoomed up almost perpendicularly to nearly 300 feet. To have tried to land there in the dark would have resulted in certain disaster. In the daylight they managed to get ashore safely and up a rough path to the cliff top. From there they made their way to Southdown Farm, where the Ford family looked after them (see Wreck No.28).

The *Westmoreland* broke up completely in a few hours and despite the efforts of coastguards, fishermen, and men from the farms roundabout, little was salved.

On the Monday, the wreck was sold by auction on the beach at Sewer Mill Cove, amid the husks of coconuts. The Kingsbridge Gazette reporter was quite impressed by the number of coconuts, which he noted "had been washing about and which had been pretty freely opened and eaten apparently in such quantity as must have severely taxed some people's digestive powers".

Auctioneer was Mr. Urell, the Chief Coastguard Officer at Hope. The wreck in the water and any cargo that might be in or under it was one lot. Some Plymouth men bought her for £110 after some spirited bidding, probably for her copper sheathing for there was little chance of any cask of rum surviving. The two other lots, masts, spars and ropes fetched a mere two pounds. Her anchors were never taken away and are just below the low water mark in the middle of the bay in which she was wrecked.

28. HALLOWEEN.
Soar Mill Cove, 1887.

BLACKADDER was the name of her ugly sister, oldest of the twins by just a few days and as black-hearted as a ship can be. But *Halloween* was the fairest of all the clipper ships in the tea trade.

Though built side by side on the banks of the River Thames to the same plans - same lines, same length, same beam and depth, the two ships somehow turned out as different as can be.

Blackadder was launched first in March, 1870 and though built like her sister, *Halloween*, to the highest requirements of Lloyds, soon earned a shocking reputation, the worst of all the China clippers. Yet *Halloween* was a beauty from the very start taking only 69 days to Sydney on her maiden voyage and then capturing the Shanghai to London record with an amazing 89 days.

The Halloween had beautiful lines. They show clearly here when she was photographed moored off Gravesend. The tug is the paddler Restless, built in 1869

On the other hand, *Blackadder* was described by one poetic soul as "rigged with curses dark" and almost immediately gained a reputation as an unlucky ship. On her first voyage both her mainmast and mizzen collapsed and she limped into Cape Town, banging into two other ships on her way. Then in the China Sea she was run into by a French steamer and only just made it into Shanghai. And so her career went on. She ran on to a reef. She lost masts in a typhoon and then nearly killed her captain when her windlass broke. On every voyage something went wrong.

Yet that unlucky ship was to survive *Halloween*, the lucky

sister, by over 18 years, finally becoming a complete loss near Bahia, now called Salvador, in Brazil.

When the two ships were launched in 1870 their lines had been set out by their owner, Captain John Willis and based on the shape and dimensions of his favourite clipper ship, *The Tweed*.

The Willis family were famous shipowners and determined men, demanding perfection from their ships and crews. John's father was known in dockland as "Old Stormy" and young John took after him. A former ship's captain himself, John Willis had his own nickname - he was called "Old Whitehat". That hat was a familiar sight as no ship of his ever set sail or returned without being personally greeted or waved goodbye. The Willises had a bad time with *Blackadder*. The underwriters queried all the mishaps to her and then refused to pay in full. John Willis's reaction was never to insure any of his ships again!

His search for perfection brought about the building of a famous ship, the *Cutty Sark*, now preserved at Greenwich. She was followed by *Blackadder* and *Halloween*. All were designed to have the same underwater shape as his beloved fast-sailing *The Tweed*. As far as *Halloween* was concerned, this meant that she 216.6 feet long and had a beam of 35.2 with a depth of 20.5. Her tonnage was 971.

The *Halloween*'s speed brought John Willis much joy and profit and he considered her luck was his luck too. But the *Halloween*'s luck started to run out in 1886. She set off from Foochow for London with a cargo of tea on that August 13, but didn't get very far before being pinned in the river by strong gales until the 19th.

When she did finally get out to sea, the wind fell away and she met nothing but light airs and long calms in the China Sea. It took 47 days for Captain R.F.Donton and his crew of 22 to beat clear to windier weather, but then those winds became constant head winds. So it wasn't until January 16,1887 that she finally reached the entrance to the Channel.

On Monday, January 17, the ship ran into that strange combination of wind and fog which all sailing men fear. And what a wind there was inside that strange blind world of fog! It was reported on land as a strong gale, a south-south-easter of Force Nine with winds of over 50 m.p.h. On the *Halloween* ,at the same time as the wind howled around them, the Second Mate on lookout reported "weather so thick we could see but a little way ahead".

At about 7.30 pm the fog lifted slightly and a light was seen on shore. Captain Donton thought that this was the Start Light. He had calculated from the course steered and the distance run that they were about eight miles off Start Point. He wasn't all that far out about their distance up Channel, but he was wildly wrong about how far they were out to sea.

Moments after the light was seen, they saw something else. Breakers shot ghostly white plumes up a dark mass before them.

There was no time to do anything. The great clipper surfed on huge waves into Sewer Mill Cove and came to a crunching stop on the seabed just 100 yards off the Priest and Clerk Rocks in the entrance to the cove. Amazingly, the impact didn't bring down her masts. But a rigging block from the mizzen mast broke free and hit the man at the wheel a savage blow on the head, spinning him unconscious into the scuppers. Not that there was any need any more for anyone at the wheel. *Halloween* was not going anywhere and huge seas started breaking right over her.

Captain Donton kept his head. Going into the wheelhouse, he jammed himself into a position where he could see his charts. There was a Coastguard station marked nearby the position in which he thought he was wrecked and he gave orders for distress rockets to be fired and flares to be lit. Much to his surprise there came no reply from the darkness. On his chart the coastguard station looked no more than half a mile away. In fact Bolt Head Coastguard Station was a mile away near Higher Sewer. But there was a coastguard lookout point a mere 1600 yards away from the wreck at Goat Point. Unfortunately, it was not continuously manned.

Finding that the rockets and flares did no good, the crew now brought out their spare clothes and bedding, soaked them in kerosene from the lamps, and set fire to them on the poop deck. A great glare pushed back the night. But there was still no response from the shore. Soon they had burnt everything they could. It seemed hopeless, so they climbed the mizzen rigging out of reach of the sea, but were sure that each wave that struck was breaking her up. The mizzen mast gave a small lurch, so they shifted to the main mast, but when that too began to shudder, they switched again to the foremast rigging. There they spent the rest of the night.

Day broke just before seven. Despite their misery, the men could now see how lucky they had been. They were at the entrance to a sandy cove, shut in on each side by precipitous cliffs. In fact they had struck the only patch of sand of any size along the five miles of cliffs from Bolt Head to Bolt Tail.

As the wind dropped, the sea started to go down, but there were still at least a hundred yards of froth and thundering surf between them and the beach. Despite this, three of the crew volunteered to swim a line ashore through the icy water. Then they planned to pull a makeshift raft of spars back and forth between ship and shore until all were safe.

The men jumped overboard in the lee of the ship which was now listing on to her port side and then struck out for the shore. First ashore was MacLean, the Second Mate, but unfortunately in the last of the breakers he lost the line. Next on to the beach was crewman Johann Wingel, but he too had lost the line. The third swimmer was a German able seaman, Gustav Lichfield. He didn't make it. The watchers on ship and shore saw him driven against the Priest and Clerk rocks. Then he floated away in the backwash, face down and obviously dead.

It was at this moment as the fog started clearing - at 7.30 am - that the ship was seen for the first time from the shore by John Ford of Southdown Farm, which is built on high ground above and to the west of the cove.

The farmer hurried down to the beach and shouted to the men on the ship to stay aboard. He had sent a man for the lifeboat. This much the men understood and settled down to wait. It was a little while later still that the coastguards at Bolt Head realised they had a ship ashore on their patch and started hauling the rocket apparatus towards Sewer Mill Cove.

The lifeboat finally arrived from Hope Cove and started taking off the exhausted crew of the *Halloween*. By the time nine of the men had jumped from the rigging into the boat, the horses pulling the rocket apparatus arrived and the coastguards fired a line across to the ship. But none of the crew would go ashore that way and in the end all were saved by the lifeboat.

Whether this was an early reflection of the crew's bitterness over the coastguards' failure to spot them during the night, it is impossible to say. But that bitterness broke out in obvious anger during the coroner's inquest into the death of Gustav Lichfield, who had died trying to swim a line ashore.

The inquest was held at Lower Sewer Farm, up in the valley to the east, on the Friday following the wreck. Lichfield's body was placed in an upstairs room so that the jury could examine it. Down below, the big farm kitchen was packed with survivors from the ship, the jurymen and coastguard officers.

First the jury viewed the body. The only mark of violence visible was a severe wound upon the forehead, which looked as though it had been caused by a projecting piece of rock. It would have been enough to have knocked the seaman out and account for his drowning.

The Coroner then called the first witness. The anger flared at once. John Jackson, the First Mate of the *Halloween* told of the death of Lichfield. Then suddenly he burst out with the efforts the crew had made to be seen: "We burned eight blue lights, fired off one rocket and lost several others...We burned fifteen gallons of paraffin oil in making flares as well as all the other oils we could get at...Flames shot up ten feet...We burned our bedding and our clothes...We got broom handles and covered them with rags and made torches..We took blue lights with us into the rigging and burned them...There was nothing to obstruct the view.." There was then a pause and into the silence he dropped a statement that was also a clear accusation: "I am

The Halloween lies wrecked between the Priest and Clark Rocks (on right) in Soar Mill Cove and the Ham Stone (background)

given to understand there was a coastguard on duty..."

Thomas Cummings, Chief Officer of the Coastguard, must have fumed as he waited to be called to give evidence. He plunged straight in. "I am the chief officer of the coastguard. And there were men on duty". Yes, the *Halloween* had come ashore at the only place on the Bolt where it would not be instantly dashed to pieces. "But though it is the best place to land, it is the worst place for being seen. You have heard that those on the ship could not see the shore. How then could those on shore see the ship?"

"They could see our lights!" interrupted the *Halloween's* Mate.

"I should say not!" retorted Cummings angrily.

It was at this moment that the Coroner, Dr. Donald Fraser of Totnes, joined in - "If they could not see the ship, surely they might have seen the signals of distress?"

Cummings obviously controlled himself to reply:"That all depends whether the man on duty happened to be patrolling near at the time. If there he might have seen. You have heard of collisions occuring at sea? It is surprising what a short distance you can see in fog or drizzle."

After this exchange, the Coroner ruled that the inquest must be adjourned until the coastguard who had been on duty, Thomas Tewkesbury, could be found and called to speak for himself.

It took nearly two hours. However, once sworn, Thomas Tewkesbury said his beat was from Starehole Bottom to the east and Down Gate to the west, a distance of some four and a half miles. He started patrolling at 5 p.m. and was on duty for seven hours. He had walked across Sewer Mill beach twice that night, both times before 7 p.m. After that he had kept to the eastward of his beat, but had been several times less than a mile from the wreck site. It had been very foggy. He had seen and heard nothing.

After Tewkesbury's evidence the Coroner summed up by saying that the Mate had given his evidence in a very explicit manner and the coastguard had been very straightforward in accounting for his time. It was clear that the coastguard on duty had not gone near the spot the wreck occurred after seven o' clock. It seemed equally clear that the nature of the ground precluded the possibility of his seeing the signals from the point at which he was later in the evening. It was for the jury to say whether anyone was to blame or not.

The jury deliberated for 15 minutes before returning their verdict: "The jury find the death of the deceased Gustav Lichfield was accidental, but they desire to express their surprise that the coastguard arrangements make it possible that a dangerous part of the coast should remain unvisited for five hours from 7p.m. to 12 midnight and they request the Coroner to call the attention of the proper authorities to the matter".

Of course, it couldn't end there. In fact before poor Gustav's body had been buried in Malborough churchyard on the Saturday afternoon, the rumours were flying wildly through the South Hams. So much so that in a sharp break with tradition - headlines in newspapers were small and conservative by comparison with today's great black type - the Dartmouth and Brixham Chronicle of January 21, 1887, daringly headed its report of the inquest: "Wreck Near Salcombe. Where Were the Coastguards?"

By then the *Halloween* lay broadside on to the cove with her back broken and her mainmast down. The work of salving the tea started, but little from the ship was undamaged. A fresh storm brought a stop to that salvage and the ship broke up. Most of the 1,600 tons of tea she carried was washed out of her and made a wall several feet high across the cove. And though the tea had been insured for £40,000, John Willis had kept his word and the ship was not insured.

A "gentleman" from London employed men to put the tea into sacks and John Ford, the farmer who had been the first to spot the wreck, was one of three local farmers contracted to cart the tea to Salcombe and put it on a small steamer and sailing vessels for London. The farmers kept their side of the bargain, but once in London, the tea and the gentlemen disappeared and no one was paid for their trouble! The tale of the missing tea fanned the gossip. "It is a long time," commented the Kingsbridge Gazette, since so much excitement has existed in the neighbourhood".

Foot Note: The remains of the *Halloween* lie 30 feet down on the seabed just 80 yards off the Priest and Clerk Rocks. You can look down on them from the western side of the Cove and at very low tides her ribs can just be spotted among the weed.

29. LINTOR KEN.
Soar Mill Cove, 1738.

A MYSTERY ship with an odd name. There are small references to her in old records, but no definite details. She is said, for example, to have been carrying cut marble blocks when sunk in Sewer Mill Cove in 1738. Fifty years later, a note appears that she was said to be carrying statues, which were salvaged and taken to Powderham for the decoration of the castle of the Courtenay family.

The story is complicated by the fact that the loss of a small Dutch vessel, the *Young Hendrick,* is recorded at Sewer Mill Cove in December 1756, and there is correspondence about this wreck between the Courtenay family and the shipowners concerning some "works of art" which were salvaged.

It may be that *Lintor Ken* wasn't the earlier ship's real name, maybe it was the best a Devon tongue could do to get around some foreign words, but there is often more than a grain of truth in these handed-down tales. Perhaps both reports were really about the same ship!

30. VOLERE.
Stanning Point, 1881.

It was Tom Hostler, the coastguard on duty at the Bolt Coastguard Station, who first found out that there was yet another wreck near Sewer Mill Cove.

At ten o'clock on the foggy morning of Sunday March 6, 1881, he heard a ship's foghorn somewhere nearby. Though the sound was distorted by the south-westerly gale and led him along some false trails, he finally spotted the sailing ship way below him, stranded on Stanning Point, just to the east of Sewer Mill Cove.

As he looked down he saw the barque's three masts were over the side and the wind-driven seas were thrusting her decking upwards from inside. He counted nine men launching a small boat and shouted to know if all aboard were safe, but received a reply which, although whipped away by the wind, didn't seem to be in English. He waved his hat to the West and pointed that way to them. He hoped they would row on towards Hope and not try landing anywhere else. They seemed to have understood him and were soon out towards the Ham Stone, well clear of the breakers and heading west.

Mr. Hostler then reported to Mr. Moore, the officer in charge of the station and messengers were sent to both Hope Cove and Salcombe lifeboat stations. Hostler then went back to the wreck.

Although he had not been away long, the ship was already breaking up. To his dismay the men in the boat were now trying to land at Sewer Mill Cove despite the huge breakers. Once again he signalled to them to go to the west and once again he thought they understood his signals.

However, the Hope lifeboat reached the wreck without meeting the men in the boat. And the Salcombe lifeboat failed to find them either. It wasn't until the next day at five a.m. that the men from the wreck were seen again - when they were picked up by a Welsh brigantine called *Ariel* seven miles west-south-west of Start Point!

They were all Italians and gave the name of their ship as *Volere,* formerly *Arproevate,* bound from Genoa to London with a cargo of 330 tons of marble in 6-ton and 14-ton blocks, and a large quantity of walnut wood on deck. They were part of a crew of 13 hands. They added that the captain and three hands were drowned. And they also said that the captain had his wife aboard and they had not seen her since the wreck.

The coastguard had no difficulty in finding her. The wife of Captain Angelo George Gavagnin was left by the tide high up in the centre of Sewer Mill Cove with one walnut log covering her feet and another her head and long dark hair. She was naked except for a pair of stockings and a white ivory cross hanging from a necklace. The cross had a little magnifying glass at its centre with a picture of a large church under it and the inscription "Chiesa di S. Antonio". On her left hand was her wedding ring and another with six diamonds. The next day the naked body of a man was washed ashore almost in the same place, but it was a member of the crew, not the captain whose body was never found.

At the inquest held by the Deputy Coroner, Mr. F. Watts, on the Wednesday in a barn at Lower Sewer Farm, there was no difficulty in identifying the body of Mrs. Gavagnin. Someone had found a photograph of the Captain and his wife taken at Truro in 1879 and there could be no doubt

31. RUPERRA.
Roden Point, 1881

THE Master lost his ticket because he went to sleep and let his ship run headlong into "something black" near dawn on January 27,1881. That something black turned out to be something very solid - the cliffs to the east of Soar Mill Cove.

Built of iron in 1877 at Jarrow, the *Ruperra*, a small steamship of 835 tons, left Alexandria on January 7,1881, with a cargo of cotton seed. She called at Gibraltar and was told to go to Hull. She left Gibraltar on January 21 and headed for the Channel. By noon on January 26, her captain, John Angel Lee, wasn't sure where he was, but thought he was off Ushant. He stopped to take soundings, decided he was definitely ten miles west of Ushant and then set off at full speed on a course which he reckoned would take him well clear of Portland Bill.

At 11p.m. he went to bed, telling the mate to report to him at midnight when they would be in sight of the Start light. The mate reported at midnight that the weather was clear, but that he had seen nothing. The master made no reply and went back to sleep. At 5 a.m. the Chief Officer, who was now in charge, saw "something very black" just ahead, stopped the engines and ordered the helm hard-a-port. He was too late. The "something black" were the huge cliffs to the east of Sewer Mill Cove and the *Ruperra* ran into them at almost her top speed.

The engines were put full astern, but had no effect. Then with the ebb tide pushing her, the steamer swung broadside to the rocks and within a few hours was broken to pieces. The crew took to the boats and, when it was light, landed at Hope. Captain Lee lost his master's ticket for six months, the first mate for three months and the second mate was reprimanded by the Court of Inquiry.

Marble blocks being salvaged in the 1920's from the Volere.

about it. Mrs.Gavagnin and the unknown seaman were both buried in Malborough Churchyard after services conducted by Abbe Rey, the Roman Catholic priest at Dartmouth.

Foot Note: Some of the marble was raised by helmet divers in the 1920s, and more was raised in 1939. The divers drilled holes in the blocks, then roped them tightly to boats or floats at low tide. As the tide rose they lifted, and then they could be pulled inshore as far as possible. The blocks would then be left high and dry when the tide went down again. It could not have been easy work, for 200 tons of marble blocks are still scattered in shallow water at the foot of the cliffs of Stanning Point just to the east of the Cove. At least one large chunk of the marble can be found on the beach in Soar Mill Cove.

The Bolt coastguard quarters are now private homes near Higher Soar.

Foot Note: The wreck is tucked in under Roden Point some 200 yards to the east of the entrance to Soar Mill Cove. She is very broken with her iron plates scattered amid copper piping and anchor chain. Divers say her two inverted compound condensing engines, which together produced 120hp, are missing, which suggests some heavy salvage, which is apparently unrecorded.

The Ham Stone. Though a magnificent sight when looking down from the cliffs above, this little 36ft-high island of rock is an obvious danger to shipping close in. There is 30 feet of water on the seaward side. No wreckage, however, lies around it. Both the wrecks it caused were towed away to sink elsewhere (see the *Soudan* Wreck No.37 and the *Herzogin Cecilie* Wreck No.38).

In the 18th century, locals said that if a couple were childless after a year of marriage, the husband should be told "to go and dig up the Ham Stone with a wooden pickaxe"!

32. MAINE.
Off the Ham Stone, 1917

THE man who sank the *Maine* - Kapitanleutnant Ralph Wenninger - hated the Dover Barrage. None of the U-boat commanders of the Flanders Flotilla liked running the gauntlet of steel mesh nets, festooned with mines at all depths, which were strung across the Straits of Dover from Folkestone to Cap Gris Nez, but Ralph Wenninger had a special reason for hating it. The Barrage had trapped him in its nets very early on in his submarine career.

He had never forgotten New Year's Day, 1916. He was then newly in command of *UC-17*. He had fouled the Dover Barrage nets in the dark and knew that his desperate forwards and backwards attempts to break the submarine free were pulling mines attached to the nets closer and closer to him. He finally broke free, but had nightmares about it for months afterwards.

He was still in command of the minelaying U-boat, *UC-17*, when, with a full cargo of 18 mines and a full load of seven torpedoes, he and two junior officers and 23 crewmen slid her out of Zeebrugge in the dark before the dawn of March 17, 1917. Once again, he had to face the nets he hated so much. But this time he went through on the surface with no problems, ran underwater after dawn down Channel, and laid some of his mines as instructed off Beachy Head.

He was then free to continue the "commercial war", as the Germans called it, which meant to them that the U-boats could sink any ship without warning if she was thought to be carrying goods or food to help the Allies' war efforts.

Fish counted, of course, as food, but Wenninger didn't waste a torpedo on his first victim, boarding the French fishing boat, *Rhodora* of 18 tons and sending her to the bottom simply by opening her sea cocks. After that he laid more mines off Newhaven, then set off down Channel in search of prey. On March 21, he fired one torpedo from a bow tube at the *Huntscape*, a steamer of 2,933 tons, but missed and she steamed away from him.

The next day he was luckier. Twenty-four miles to the east of Start Point, he found a big New Zealand steamer, the 11,140-ton *Rotorua*. One seaman died as the torpedo slammed into her side and she sank swiftly. Wenninger was no doubt jubilant at the sinking of such a big ship. He could not know, however, that the sinking of the *Roturua* would push the total of Allied losses for that March past the 100-ship mark and set a grim record for the losses in a single month. The U-boats were, in fact, bringing Britain close to defeat. And Wenninger and his colleagues had not finished yet...

She was a dirty British cargo-ship with a salt-caked smokestack and she came zigzagging down the Channel on a mad March day. She was the *Maine*, a 3,616-ton steamer, which had left London's East India Dock at nine in the morning of Wednesday, March 21, 1917, bound for Philadelphia. In her holds was a very unimportant cargo of 500 tons of chalk, and 50 tons of general stores, including cowhair, horsehair, goatskins, and fenugreek seeds which farriers use as medicine for horses. But though her cargo for this

This picture of the Maine was taken in 1912 when she was still called the Sierra Blanca.

outward voyage was not a very profitable one, her owners, the Atlantic Transport Company, had high hopes of a valuable war supplies cargo for her return run to Britain.

By the morning of Friday, March 23, the *Maine* was well down Channel. On board were a crew of 43. On the bridge was Captain W."Bill" Johnston and his First Officer. Down below, the negro cook was serving breakfast to the men off watch. Those on watch included special lookouts on the forecastle head and the poop and the 4.7 inch gun on the poop was manned, for there was no doubt in the mind of anyone aboard that the *Maine* was now well and truly in one of the U-boats' favourite killing grounds. The constant zigzagging was obvious reminder of that, for each zigzag meant a lurch and roll at the turn.

That Friday morning, the weather was uncertain. Though the sea was fairly calm, every few minutes a heavy shower would come from the scudding clouds and sweep across the deck before racing away across the sea and obscuring the distant line of land. At 8 a.m., the *Maine* was 13 miles south of Berry Head, steering a magnetic course of South 89 degrees, a course that would keep her well clear of the South Devon coast. Whether she should have been there is open to doubt. There would be talk later that she was entering a prohibited zone - a British minefield - and was well off the course that had been laid down for her. The British mines were there to catch any German submarines planning to lay mines in the Dartmouth approaches.

At 8.05 a.m. the question of whether the *Maine* was on or off course ceased to matter. The rain squalls churning up the surface had given Ralph Wenninger in *UC-17* the perfect cover for his approach to the solitary steamer. He fired one torpedo from a bow tube while still at periscope depth.

That torpedo struck the merchantman full in the port side, level with No. 2 hold. The blast knocked Captain "Bill" Johnston off his feet, blew off the hatches of No. 2 and No. 3 holds, smashed the port gig and wrecked the bridge. And it made a great hole in her side through which water poured on to her cargo of chalk, horsehair and goatskins.

Captain Johnston could feel her settling by the head and immediately turned her bow towards the land. His distress calls were swiftly answered.

First help to arrive was a Royal Navy torpedo boat, No. 99, commanded by Lieutenant-Commander Percy Taylor of the R.N.R. He had been in command of a flotilla of minesweepers, busy clearing mines from the entrances to Dartmouth and Teignmouth – some of which had probably been the last six carried by *UC-17* – and had just started on his way home to Devonport.

Commander Taylor put his ship alongside the *Maine*, which had stopped when her engines flooded, and took off most of the crew. Captain Johnston told him that his ship was now completely out of action with the midships fully flooded, but the Commander thought there might be a chance of beaching her in Bigbury Bay, probably Hope Cove, and passed a towline to the stricken ship. Other patrol boats now arrived and took on the tow too, but progress was very slow.

At noon the first tug arrived and took over the tow. It was too late. Soon after the new tow was established, the *Maine*'s internal bulkheads collapsed and at 12.45 p.m. she sank. She did so in Commander Taylor's words: "Gracefully, upright and on an even keel". She was just a mile offshore. As she did so, Oberleutnant Wenninger headed his submarine away to the north-east, heading homeward for Zeebrugge, and the Bruges base of the Flanders Flotilla.

Captain Johnston and his crew were landed at Plymouth and caught the train to London the next morning to report to the owners, the Atlantic Transport Company at their headquarters at 38, Leadenhall Street. As they sat in

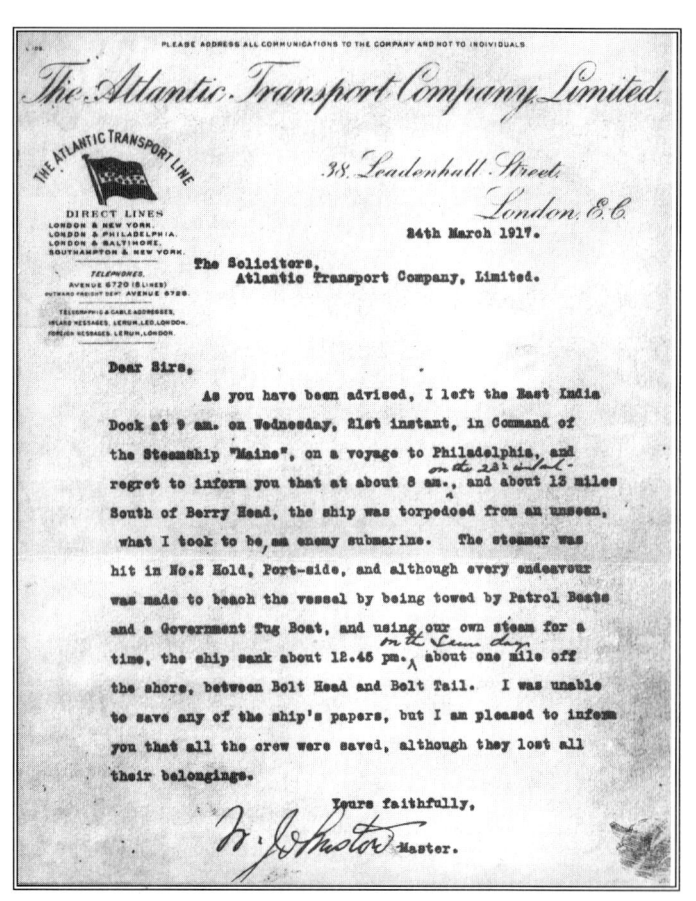

The letter written by Captain Johnston to the Maine's owners reporting her loss.

the train, the negro cook leaned over and gave Captain Johnston a "souvenir" of the sinking. It was the rudder of the torpedo which had sunk their ship and the cook had picked it up from the deck after the explosion.

That little rudder came in very useful. At one stage during his meeting with the owners, it was suggested that the *Maine* was not sunk by a torpedo, but by a mine as Captain Johnston had steered the wrong course and entered a British minefield. At this moment Captain Johnston produced the torpedo's rudder - and there was no more talk of mines or wrong courses! Captain Johnston continued his merchant navy career and survived the war.

Wenninger, too, survived the war, but not until after his worst nightmare came true. He was sunk by a mine when going through the Dover Barrage on April 22, 1918. He and 20 of his men got to the surface in bubbles of air when they opened the hatches of the crippled submarine lying on the seabed 100 feet down. Only six men survived, one of whom was Wenninger. He spent the rest of the war in a British prison camp for officers at Donnington Hall, Leicestershire, but by 1929 was the executive officer of the German cruiser *Berlin*.

For a long time the Maine's position was quite clear. Her two masts stuck up 12 feet clear of the surface and the Admiralty issued a Notice to Mariners about this hazard. In time both her masts collapsed and, for some reason known only to themselves, the fishermen of Hope and Salcombe called her "the Railway Line Wreck" (could it have been some dreadful joke about Maine Line?).

Foot Note: You can see the grave of the *Maine* if you look out over the Ham Stone and spot a cluster of small boats and big inflatables. You will see these dive boats almost every day because this is one of the most dived wrecks in Britain. She is so popular with divers because she is easily accessible and is still a very ship-like ship, upright and on an even keel on the shingle seabed at 121 feet, with 65 feet from the surface to her deck Almost the whole ship can be seen on one dive because of the extraordinarily clear water around her.

The *Maine* was built for the Sierra Shipping Co of Liverpool and was called *Sierra Blanca* when launched in January,1905. She was 375ft overall, 361ft between perpendiculars as she had an overhanging counter stern of 14 feet. Her beam is 46.2ft. She was renamed in 1913 when bought by the Atlantic Transport Co.

She was first dived in 1961 by Torbay BSAC, who bought her for £100 and salvaged her bronze prop for which they received £840. Then the gun was salvaged off her stern. And in 1983 another diving team from Torbay BSAC raised the spare iron propellor off her deck, and you can see it today displayed at the front of the Victoria Shopping Centre, Paignton.

It is interesting to add, in this area noted for the number of Albert Medals awarded at shipwrecks(see Wrecks Nos 22 and 63), that an Albert Medal was won aboard the *Maine*. Lieutenant-Commander Arthur Warden was presented with his medal by King George V for his "special gallantry" in going into the holds of the *Maine* at Bassin Loubet, Boulogne, on October 26,1915, and using a fire-hose to put out a fire among the cases of high explosive with which the ship was packed. Commander Warden later retired and settled in Devon.

33. CANTABRIA.
Steeple Cove, 1932.

IF a naked woman stands at the bow of a ship in a storm then the high winds die away. Every sailor knows that - which is why in olden days the figureheads of ships were of women with at least one naked breast.

But that sort of good luck superstition is rare at sea compared with the list of things that will bring bad luck to the seafarer.

For example, every sailor knows that Friday is a bad day to start a voyage, that it is unlucky to change the name of a ship, that whistling will bring a gale, that the loss overboard of a bucket or mop will bring misfortune, and a voyage will

S.S. CANTABRIA ASHORE NEAR SALCOMBE

The final piece of bad luck. The Cantabria wrecked in Steeple Cove.

end in disaster if a barefoot woman crosses the path of a crewman on his way to join his ship...

Captain Josef Learreta of the Spanish steamer *Cantabria* had his mind on the voyage ahead of him to Newcastle with a cargo of iron ore when he walked down to his ship in the harbour of Bilbao in the early morning of Thursday, December 1, 1932. He saw the woman carrying nets to mend cross his path from the little fishing boat moored near his own 1803-ton merchantman. It was only after she had passed that he noticed she had bare feet, but didn't regard it as an omen of bad luck. That came later.

The 263-foot-long *Cantabria* sailed that Thursday afternoon and the 23 superstitious Spanish sailors aboard were relieved that it wasn't a Friday. However, for Juan Almego, one of the ordinary seamen aboard, the bad luck started quickly. He slipped and fell and when they got him up it was clear that his arm was broken. Captain Learreta cursed, but put back into port to put the man ashore. It was five minutes into Friday when their voyage started again.

Three days out the cook's help lost a bucket and mop overboard. No one said anything, but they were not surprised when the same kitchen hand was nearly crushed to death when the top section of the aft mast suddenly broke off and crashed to the deck beside him.

However, they had good weather for most of the passage. It was cold of course, but the nights were clear and Captain Learreta was able to pick up the lighthouses with ease. Or could until Monday, December 12, when he entered the Channel. A few wisps of mist came first. Then in less than an hour he needed all his lights on. From that moment on he was in the densest fog recorded in the whole of that decade. He looked in vain for the charted lights, but could not see even a glimmer. In fact he could not see his own stern, just a glow somewhere in the murk behind him.

Then his ship started rising and falling over big swells. It wasn't exactly rough, but it added to the eerie feeling. Captain Learreta couldn't even see the surface of the sea from the bridge, but his stomach told him that the swells were really big. Though of course he didn't know it then, all the reports from shipping of that fog, which blacked out the whole of the English Channel and Southern England, spoke of the unusually big swells which seemed to come up with the clamp-down of the fog. Reports in newspapers of the fog are festooned with near misses at sea, at least two collisions, and numerous strandings.

Captain Learreta himself said later, though an interpreter, that at one time he could hear at least three foghorns near him. One ship came very close indeed, and though he felt he could almost touch her and was slopped by her wash, he saw nothing. But, believing he had a great deal of sea room, when the fog signals faded away, he continued his slow progress up the Channel.

As the night passed the fog, if anything, seemed to get thicker. It was so thick that when the *Cantabria* hit the inner part of the reef called the Gregory Rocks, which lies underwater between the Hamstone and Bolt Head, the first the captain and crew knew about it was a great jolt followed by a booming ripping noise. Then she came free and churned on into Steeple Cove and ran into more rocks which lie right under the two rock pinnacles on shore at the western end of the cove. Steeple Cove starts at the unmanned coastguard hut on the cliffs at the eastern end.

The *Cantabria* came to a halt at precisely 3.15 a.m. It was the 13th! They were 13 days out! The captain had been crossed by a barefoot woman! Their voyage had started on a Friday! All their talk of misfortune after the loss of the bucket and mop had come true!

In fact, they were actually quite lucky. The *Cantabria* was perched safely on the rocks, driven hard home, and though she heeled a little she stayed upright. Despite this, the sound of the swell on the rocks around them and the water inside her caused some sort of panic. They abandoned ship as fast as they could. But not before Captain Learreta made sure that his radio officer had sent off an S.O.S.

The records of the Lands End radio station show that the distress signal was received at 3.31 a.m. Hope Cove coastguards were the first to be informed and they passed the message on to Salcombe lifeboat station. At 4.30 a.m. the maroons soared up and exploded to call out the lifeboat's crew and the *Alfred and Clara Heath* was under way by 5 a.m. Even so, the fog and the fact that they had been given only a rough position for the wreck, made their progress very slow.

All 24 men of the *Cantabria* had now got themselves ashore in the ship's boat. They were only 80 yards from their ship in under the cliffs. One of the crew - one of the few aboard who could speak English - told the reporter from the Kingsbridge Gazette: "**We had no time to get our clothing for we felt the ship heeling over. We soon got to shore and had to hold on to rocks. Everyone got ashore all right, but the worst part was that we had little or no clothes. Some of the men had only felt slippers on their feet and little to wear. Others had only the thin overalls we wear in the engine room. One of the fellows had some cigarettes which we shared. We were soon soaked to the skin by the thick fog and mist. Cold, hungry and frightened, we clung to the rock just out of the water, keeping our spirits up by cheery talk for we didn't know where we were. However in**

the early light the lifeboat suddenly came out of the fog".

Eddy Distin, the cox'n of the Salcombe lifeboat, found the steamer, moored up alongside, and then discovered there was no one aboard. It was only when the lifeboat closed the cliffs that they found the crew huddled under an overhang. The cliff couldn't be climbed there and so the lifeboat would have to take them all off. But there was no way that Eddy Distin was going to risk his boat in the ground swell among the rocks. In the end by using the *Cantabria*'s boat as a ferry, they had all the Spaniards aboard and back in Salcombe by 8 a.m. Distin reported that the steamer looked to him like a total loss. He thought her back was broken and the iron ore was washing out of a gaping hole in her starboard side.

It was left to one of her crew to point out that the ship had been doomed all the time for her name had been changed not once, but twice! She had been both the *Corgrag* and then the *Hornsey* before becoming the *Cantabria*. She stayed on the rocks for a while, but then someone whistled during salvage work - and up came a gale! The seas on the Bolt during a gale are not kind and the Spanish steamer was soon completely out of luck and sight. **Foot Note:** There was little salvage and her iron propellor and her plating are all there underwater just to the right of the pinnacle nearest to the path.

34. AMELIE-SUZANNE. Off Cove, 1972.

DURING the foggy night of March 31-April 1, 1972, this Belgian MFV went on the rocks at the eastern point of Off Cove, the biggest bay in the cliffline before Bolt Head. Following their May-Day call, the crew of five were rescued by Salcombe lifeboat. Soon after, the fishing vessel slipped deeper and broke up. At very low tides part of her wreckage can still be seen.

The Amelie-Suzanne was smashed to pieces in Off Cove in 1972.

SECTION FOUR –
Bolt Head to Prawle Point.

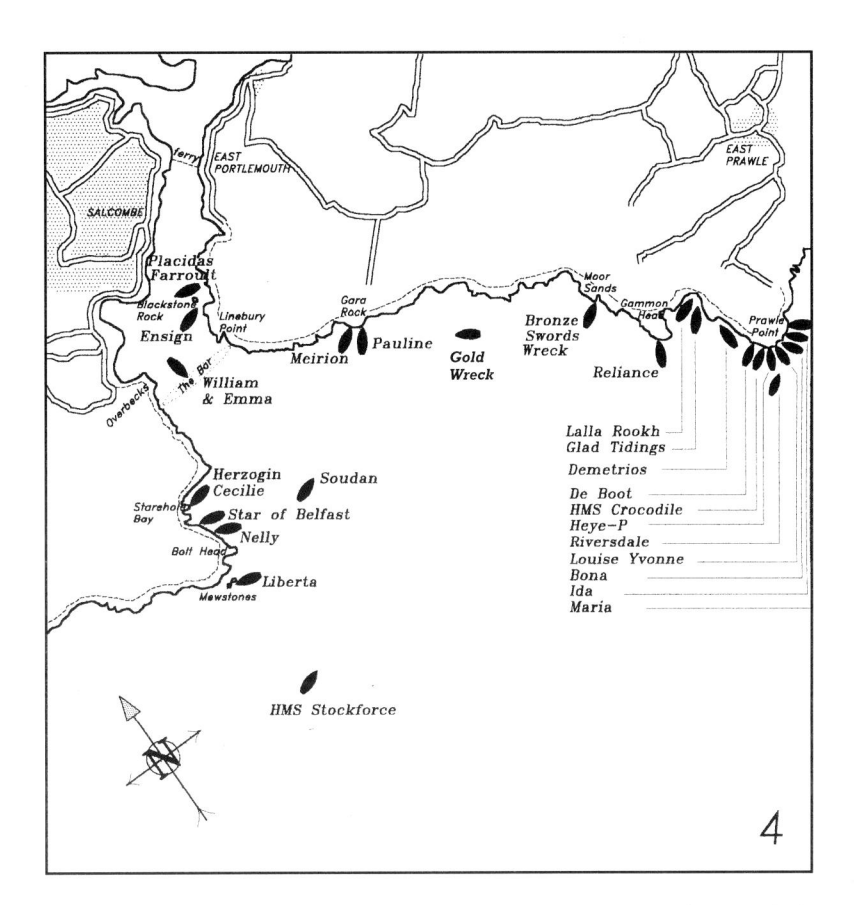

35. HMS STOCKFORCE.
Off Bolt Head, 1918.

A "SPECIAL Service Ship" was how the Navy desribed her in their records, but in fact she was a Q-ship. This 732-ton small coastal steamer had, until the beginning of 1918, been the *Charyce*. The Navy requisitioned her in Cardiff and fitted her with two four-inch guns, a 12-pounder and a 3-pounder, all hidden behind screens, which looked like ordinary deck housings. Her captain was Lieutenant Harold Auten.

On July 30, 1918, *Stockforce* was steaming along innocently to the west when Kapitanleutnant Oelricher in *UB-98* put a torpedo into her. It struck on the starboard side putting the hidden forward gun out of action and wounding four of her crew. The make-believe abandon ship party, showing all the right signs of panic, then launched their boat and rowed desperately away from the ship. Meanwhile the hidden Navy gun crews lay at their stations waiting for the submarine to surface even though water was pouring into *Stockforce* between decks.

After five minutes *UB-98* surfaced, but lay half-a-mile off for another 15 minutes waiting for any suspicious move. Finally she moved in to just 300yds away. As she did so, the Q-ship dropped her screens and opened fire with both four-inch guns. The first round carried away one of the periscopes. The second shot hit the conning-tower dead centre, blowing it away and sent the man in it high in the air. Another shot hit the submarine where the conning tower had been and just below the waterline. Blue smoke poured out of the sub as round after round hit her. After 20 hits the U-boat sank by the stern.

The *Stockforce* was in a bad way and Captain Auten headed for land as fast as he could, but the ship was awash forward and was clearly unlikely to travel far. However, after transferring half the crew and the wounded to a trawler, the *Stockforce* got within a short distance of Bolt Head before sinking.

Lieutenant Auten was awarded the Victoria Cross and there were decorations for most of the crew. But amazingly, the *UB-98* managed to make her way home and was handed over to the Royal Navy at the end of the war by Kapitanleutnant Oelricher when the surviving U-boats surrendered at Harwich!

36. LIBERTA.
Mewstones, Salcombe. 1926.

THE siren blew mournfully, but insistently from somewhere outside the entrance to Salcombe Harbour. Despite the weather Pilot Chant in the little town on the hillside further up the estuary knew that he had to answer the call. Or try to.

As he struggled down to his motorboat, the westerly wind crackled the rain across his oilskins. The wind and the rain were bad enough - and he had doubts too about the possibility of crossing the Bar - but it was the third element of the weather which made his journey almost impossible on that rotten night of Sunday, February 14, 1926. For the whole of the South Devon coast was wrapped in fog and nowhere was the blanket thicker than in the Salcombe

Came the dawn - and the Liberta was balanced on a rock amidships.

Estuary. No matter how much the wind increased, the fog seemed to stay still.

By the time Pilot Chant had got past the ruins of the old castle, whose shape he sensed rather than saw, and had found the Wolf Rock Buoy more by luck than judgement, his boat was bucking and pitching so much that he knew the seas over the Bar would be impossible. They were the kind of seas which in 1916 had capsized the Salcombe lifeboat, the *William and Emma*, on the Bar, drowning 13 of her 15 crew (see Wreck No.39).

But Chant pushed on a little further towards the siren's call, before the white of breaking seas told him that his mission was truly impossible. As he turned back, he hoped that the ship calling for a pilot would stand well off until the fog cleared, the siren suddenly stopped. It was just coming up to nine p.m.

As the pilot made his way back up the estuary and passed South Sands bay, so Tom Dickenson of the South Sands Garage settled himself in the warm room in front of his transmitter for a pleasant hour or two of chat to fellow radio "hams" around the world. Tom Dickenson's call-sign was "Six D.I." and he was an experienced wireless operator having been on the Post Office staff and stationed at Bolt Head during the First World War.

But no sooner had his set warmed up than it was spilling out the loudest and closest S.O.S. that Tom Dickenson had ever heard...."S.O.S...Liberta....We do not know where we are aground...Want help..." From the strength of that signal and from his aerial readings, Tom Dickenson placed the wreck as somewhere between Hope Cove and Start Point. He rang the coastguard.

The coastguard at Prawle Point could narrow the area. "Steamer ashore in vicinity Bolt Head. Wind south-west moderate. Squally. Dense fog. Sea moderate." was the entry in their log. And now as the lifeboat at Salcombe had been removed as "not needed" the previous October, the Hope Cove lifeboat, *Alexandra*, was launched. Conditions for that launch at Hope were terrible with villagers standing up to their waists in the sea before they could get her off. Once clear of Bolt Tail they were in the full force of the wind. Their sails were of little use and they settled down to a six-mile row. It was to take them four hours.

Back in Salcombe, Tom Dickenson was acting as a central clearing station, relaying messages and passing on information he was now picking up from all along the English coast. No one was yet sure where *Liberta* was. Niton and Penzance were picking up her signals and a French radio station gave her position as "west of Plymouth". Brixham coastguards were told that she was in the "vicinity of Start" and as a result, the powerful Brixham lifeboat, a 40-footer with a 45 h.p. engine, was launched to aid the search.

At dawn the fog lifted. At the same time the wind increased to a full gale. It was now clear to the exhausted crew of the Hope lifeboat and to those on the cliffs that the siren which they had originally thought was calling for a pilot, in fact had been a distress signal.

For now they could see her. The 376-foot-long steamer *Liberta* was jammed between the Mewstones at the foot of Bolt Head and all around her was white water studded with the black heads of rocks. As each wall of water, driven by the gale, surged over her, even bigger rocks showed for a second and then were gone. She seemed to be balanced on one particularly large rock amidships and nodded like a massive rocking-horse as each new wave hit her.

Despite the broken water and the rocks, the *Alexandra* tried to get close enough to shout to the skipper, but it was impossible. The lifeboat pulled back to wait for full light. As she did so, the lifeboat from Brixham arrived and the two lifeboats, side by side, rode out the last of the dark.

This withdrawal obviously alarmed the crew of the *Liberta* and they began firing flares. Later William Sanders, coxswain of the Brixham boat was quoted by the local paper: "**We tried to tell them that we would do all we could for them, but they did not understand. So then I took a risk and managed to get a line aboard, but the seas were running so hard that I found the greatest difficulty in keeping her steady and at last the line carried away as we surged. Finally I was able to get a second line aboard and then a breeches buoy and endeavoured to get the crew to** let themselves be drawn across the raging seas.

Eventually they grasped what was wanted of them and we got three of the crew into the lifeboat. At that moment the Hope rocket team got a line across and the rest of the crew of 30 decided to be brought ashore that way. And I don't blame them!"

Last man ashore was Captain Achille Moscatilli. He told his rescuers that his 4073-ton steamer was on her way from La Spezia to Rotterdam in water ballast to pick up a cargo of coal to take back to Italy. During the voyage they had been in bad weather and poor visibility for ten days. On the Sunday, they had taken soundings at frequent intervals. All had given depths of well over 20 fathoms so they thought they were well south of their proper course, whereas in fact they were too far to the north. When the fog came down they were completely lost.

The *Liberta*, which had been built by Barclay Curle of Glasgow in 1900, had previously sailed under the name of *Vermont*. From the point of view of the rocket rescuers, she could not have ended up in a better place. She was broadside on just 170 yards from the foot of the cliff and the first rocket from Bolt Head fell straight across her radio aerial. It was not easy for the crew to haul the breeches buoy up so high with two men at a time, but the Hope crew worked so well that even the ship's mascot - "a splendid dog" - and the ship's cat were brought ashore. Times have not changed - the dog was promptly quarantined under the Rabies Act!

The Italians fared better. The local paper reported fulsomely that: **"Lady Clementine Waring of the Moult sent a message that everybody was to be brought to her residence. Here the men found a real British welcome awaited them, being received by her Ladyship, her daughter and several guests. The men were made comfortable with food, clothing, cigarettes and tobacco, which they fully appreciated. Lady Clementine was to have attended a dinner in London on Monday evening, but she cancelled her engagement, preferring to entertain the shipwrecked mariners. The motors at the door were already loaded with luggage, when Lady Clementine decided to stay and entertain her guests".**

Four days after she struck, the steamer broke completely in half. The rock on which she had perched amidships with her bow out of the water at low tide had caused most of the break; the gale had done the rest. She had, in fact, run in between the Little Mewstone and the shore and ended up between both Mewstones, the Little and the Great. After she broke in two, the halves lay for some time just 150 feet apart. The *Liberta*'s owners, Corrado and Parodi of Genoa, asked for salvage to be attempted, but in the end little was saved. Soon after breaking in half, she sank from view.

The Liberta broke cleanly in two only four days after she first struck.

Divers have found her plating spread around in the weed on the rocks and her boilers sit in the middle of an area of sand.

Foot Note: There are "Mewstones" all around our coasts. "Mew" was an old English word for a gull. The cat-like mewing noises gulls often make has probably got something to do with it. Mewstones are rocks particularly used by gulls. The Mewstones at Salcombe are usually packed with them. Or if they are not there you can certainly see that they have been!

37. SOUDAN.
Salcombe entrance, 1887

THIS small French steamer of 844 tons first came to grief some distance from her present position near the entrance to Salcombe. In fact she hit the Ham Stone in thick fog in the morning of June 27, 1887, when carrying a cargo of peanuts, hides, and oil, together with eight passengers and 24 crew.

When the fog lifted, the eight passengers were taken off by a yacht, and the *Soudan* was seen to be firmly seated on the outer ledge of the Ham Stone with 12ft of water in her foreholds. At 6pm the tugs *Vixen* and *Raleigh* were standing by.

As the tide rose, the *Soudan* floated free or "glided towards the mainland" as the Lloyds agent put it. By 10pm she was well afloat, though deep by the head, and the tugs started towing her towards Salcombe. She proved almost unmanageable and progress was slow.

At midnight when they were a little to the west of the entrance to Salcombe, it was clear that the water was gaining fast. Suddenly the engine-room bulkhead broke, and as the tugs slipped their hawsers, she gave a sort of plunge forward and sank. At 3am her main topmast was still visible above the water, and her cargo was starting to float out of her.

Not that she was abandoned. Salvage steamers tried to raise her for two months by all sorts of methods - by chains around her, by air bags and by blowing air into her ballast tanks. But nothing worked, and she is now in the same place.

Foot Note: Her wreck is very popular with divers and if you look out from the coastguard lookout on Bolt Head and slightly inwards towards the entrance to Salcombe, you will usually have no difficulty in spotting her position because of the dive boats over her. Some idea of how often she is dived comes from the fact that the brass boss of the propellor shaft behind the iron propellor is always polished – by divers' hands! If the divers aren't there, you may see a buoy over her - one of the Salcombe yacht club race marks is sometimes placed almost on top of the wreck!

38. HERZOGIN CECILIE.
Starehole Bay, 1936.

THEY called her "The Duchess". And Duchess she was as she swished across the world's oceans at her top speed of over 20 knots. This was not quite a world record – the Yankee clipper James Baines held that with 21 knots. The real reason for calling her "The Duchess" was because of her figurehead, which was of the Duchess Cecilie, daughter of the Duke of Oldenburg.

A 3,111-ton four-master, the *Herzogin Cecilie* was launched in Bremerhaven, Germany, in April, 1902 and at first she was the crack cadet-training ship of Norddeutscher Lloyd. Then in World War One she was interned in Chile. At the end of the war, she was handed over to the French Government, who sold her to a Finnish shipping firm. It was then that she really showed what she could do. During the great grain races, she left them all standing, which is not surprising because when she had all sails spread, she had an acre of canvas up aloft. With all that pushing along her 336ft hull, which was only 46ft wide, she smashed her way from Australia to England in under 90 days. In one run from Melbourne to Taltal in Chile, she managed 2120 nautical miles in seven days – a sailing record that has never been equalled.

The Herzogin Cecilie under full sail.

Though the *Herzogin Cecilie* will never sail again, we do know what it was like on board her at full speed for her Mate, Elis Karlsson, wrote about it and described what happened when a gale hit her:

"The hands had barely finished their tasks when it hit us. The deep tone in the rigging rose suddenly to a brutal howl and the deck under my feet gave a jerk as if the ship had stumbled; then she leapt ahead. The day was swept away and twilight descended with the hail-filled wind, and the surface of the sea was beaten into smoky spume. The smaller, irregular wave formations were flattened or torn to shreds; the big West-wind rollers, too mighty to be flattened even by such a wind, rose steeper at their crests and hurried their pace.

"For some moments the ship kept up with the seas. On the wind-flattened ridge, with surging white water up to her rails as if in a huge foam-bath, she stormed along with a crumbling avalanche of breaking crest under her, her jib-boom pointing into the valley below and ahead.

"Slowly she lost the race as the undertow made itself felt, and her bows were lifted by the shoulder of the sea; for a while she lingered on the windward slope, her jib-boom thrusting at the screaming murk; slowly she sank down into the comparative

April 24, 1936, she left Falmouth for Ipswich. The night was dark with rain, and a moderate south-westerly kept her running free. At midnight the wind dropped and the rain became fog. The *Herzogin Cecilie* moved on over the light swell and her manual foghorn sounded every two minutes. At 3am the night broke, but the fog remained. Suddenly Captain Sven Eriksson saw a dark line through the fog. He had no doubts: "Hard a-starboard!". It was too late.

The Mate, Elis Karlsson, later described it like this: *"The ship lifted, then struck again with a sickening thud; then the swell lifted her again and she drifted away from the hump or rock ahead and broadside on, current or swell carried her towards a steep cliff on our port side. The Captain ordered me to let go both anchors; the ship took ground perhaps a cable-length from the cliff."*

She had in fact hit the Ham Stone off Soar Mill Cove. Holed in the forepeak, she settled by the head. The Salcombe lifeboat soon arrived and the captain asked them to take off a woman passenger and 21 of the crew. Eight stayed – the captain and his wife, the two mates, and four crewmen. By afternoon a rocket line had been fired from

The figurehead of "The Duchess"

quiet of the valley, which echoed with the turmoil above, where the hail-mixed spindrift beat a frenzied tattoo on the straining canvas.

"Every now and then I glanced at the helmsmen and eventually it dawned on me that they hardly moved the wheels. And yet the ship was definitely on course, dead before the wind. She had not time to roll in her headlong rush to eastward and she was sailing herself!...I knew then that nothing would carry away; nothing would stop this marvellous ship in this her hour; she was part of the elements; as she was carried eastward in the heart of the gale, ship and the elements were one".

That took place on the Duchess's last voyage. It was a fast one, her fastest ever in fact, Australia to Falmouth in 86 days. But at 8pm on

She struck the Ham Stone and then drifted in towards the cliffs.

the cliffs and a breeches buoy was in operation. Ashore went sails and rope. Down came the top-gallant and royal yards and off they went to Salcombe. Small coasters shifted 450 tons of undamaged grain. But the rest of her cargo was already swelling and pushing up the deck in places. Those left aboard were not cheered to learn that 100yds astern of them lay the bones of another clipper, *Halloween* (see Wreck No.28). It looked then as though the *Herzogin Cecilie* was going to join her.

But, suddenly, there was a chance she could be saved. A group of well-wishers put up the money to save the famous ship and to pay for towing her in to Salcombe. Once there the damaged cargo could be removed, the holes sealed and she could be fully repaired in dry dock in Plymouth. And it is likely that she would have been, except for local opposition to taking her into Salcombe itself. The stench of rotting wheat would, it seems, do nothing for the holidaymakers. And so it was agreed to put her into Starehole Bay until all the wheat was taken out of her.

On June 19, 1936, with the help of pumps and crews from Plymouth Dockyard, the Duchess came up from her rocky couch. Then with two tugs pulling and a spring tide helping, the ship was towed round to Starehole Bay and allowed to settle gently on a sandy bed. Unfortunately, no one knew how thin that sandy mattress was. Underneath the sand lay a very rocky base.

A rope bridge was rigged from ship to shore and volunteers, largely Cambridge University students, started getting the wet mass of wheat out of her. They did well, reducing the original cargo of 4250 tons to just over 1000. But as they worked so did the ship. She worked herself down through the sand nearly four metres to the solid rock and poised herself amidships.

On July 18, a south-easterly gale sent a swine of a swell surging into the bay. Elis Karlsson knew then that she was finished: **"We stood listening to rivets snapping with reports like pistol shots; the ship was working heavily in the swell and had reached rock. Staunchions between the decks bent and buckled. It was the end."**

The wreck was sold to a Kingsbridge metal dealer, Messrs Noyce, for £225, but she did not go all at once. The ship stayed upright with her masts still up for months. Then the sea came back to finish the job, almost 11 months after her wrecking. This storm broke her up. Her masts crashed down and overnight she was just a dark shape underwater.

Foot Note: She has, of course, broken even more since then. Some of her is buried under the sand, but the dark shape you can see as you look down on the northern end of Starehole Bay from

The Herzogin Cecilie in Starehole Bay with the grain oozing out and staining the water around her.

A swine of a swell started to break her up.

the path is caused by the kelp and other weeds growing on the bow locker and the ribs and plating. At her deepest, the wreck is just 20 feet below the surface and is home to some big conger eels. The bow points out to sea and there is anchor chain leading away to seaward.

If you walk the path at a time of extreme low water on spring tides, you can see the tip of the bow section poking out of the water. Because of this danger to boats, she is often buoyed. This is another wreck much frequented by divers because it is a pretty dive for beginners and is in sheltered water and can be dived when other wrecks cannot be reached because of bad weather. You will see diving boats over her at most times.

There have been other wrecks in Starehole Bay (originally Stair Hole because of the track up which seaweed was carried to manure the fields of East Soar

The hospital ship Asturias beached in Starehole Bay after being torpedoed by the German submarine UC-66.

Farm). The *Star of Belfast* was wrecked there on December 18, 1847. She was bound for Antigua from London with general cargo. The captain was the only man saved. And on July 24, 1852, the *Nelly*, a smack, was wrecked there. She was attempting to land smuggled goods!

At the seaward end of Starehole Bottom, where there is said to have been an ancient Danish settlement, are inlets or small coves which in the 18th century were called "gamps" The first to the west is Old Gamp, then Middle Gamp and the third to the eastermost is the New Gamp.

It was in front of Middle Gamp that the First World War hospital ship *Asturias* was beached in Starehole Bay after being torpedoed five miles south of the Start by Oberleutnant Herbert Pustkuchen in *UC-66* on March 21, 1916.

The *Asturias* had disembarked wounded from Salonica at Avonmouth and was on passage up Channel. She had all her lights on and a big Red Cross on each side, which were floodlit. The torpedo's explosion killed 35 crew and medical staff aboard. The wounded were brought ashore and nursed at Overbecks.

The *Asturias* was later refloated and went back into service. Pustkuchen and his crew were killed in June that year when he was detected by the listening gear of the Lizard Hydrophone Division, which guided warships to the U-boat. Their depth charges detonated *UC-66*'s cargo of mines and "the sea boiled over".

If you follow the path on to the Edwardian house called Overbecks, which is a National Trust property with the magnificent gardens of Sharpitor around it, you will be able to see some relics of the "Duchess" in the museum there, even the heads of pitchforks, used to move the cargo and found by divers in the wreckage. The museum is open from Easter to the end of October. The Sharpitor gardens are open all year round.

Further on, in Salcombe itself, you will find the Salcombe Maritime Museum squeezed into the old council hall at the

A sad man and his sad wife. Captain Sven Eriksson of the Herzogin Cecilie and his wife, Pamela, wait at the Ferry Inn steps in Salcombe for a lift back to their stricken ship.

foot of Market Street where it joins Fore Street. The Museum, opposite the Post Office, houses the most wonderful collection of shipwreck and other maritime material.

Don't miss it - relics from most of the shipwrecks of the South Hams are on display here. For example, one of the oars and part of the woodwork of the *William and Emma* lifeboat (see Wreck No.39), a swivel gun from the Erme mouth wrecks (see Wreck No.1), silver and bronze lifeboat medals (see Wreck No.11), are all on view. The Museum is open in the mornings and then again each afternoon from April to October.

39. WILLIAM AND EMMA.
Salcombe Bar, 1916.

A NARROW steep shallow sandbank, simply called The Bar, has built up across the mouth of the Salcombe Estuary, which by the way is not an estuary at all, for no great rivers feed it, but really a drowned inlet, though a very pretty one.

The Bar is a major hazard to shipping in onshore winds between east and south, particularly during ebb tides, when there can be as little as two feet of water over it. Walkers on the path can not fail to see the troubled water at these times when the seas break along it.

The Admiralty Pilot underlines the danger : **"The navigation of this bar constitutes the greatest trouble in making the entrance, as there is frequently, especially in southerly winds, a breaking swell over it, and in such conditions craft even of the lightest draught should not attempt the entrance till at least half flood. In southerly gales, the sea breaks over the bar with violence, and in these circumstances the entrance should not on any account be attempted"**.

The Bar has been responsible for many capsizes, but none have had such terrible consequences as that of the Salcombe lifeboat, the *William and Emma* on October 27, 1916.

The lifeboat was called out at 5.12 a.m. by Prawle coastguards who reported the Plymouth schooner *Western Lass* was ashore at Langerstone Point, east of Prawle, and another schooner, the *Traveller,* was ashore near the Start. Both were in need of assistance.

A heavy south-westerly gale was blowing, but the 15 men in the lifeboat still went. The seas on the Bar were horrendous, but Cox'n Samuel Distin took the boat through them and they rowed safely to the open sea where reefed sails took them to the east. When they were out of sight another telephone message was given to the secretary of the lifeboat. It came from Prawle saying that their rocket team had managed to save the crew of the *Western Lass* by breeches buoy, and the crew of the *Traveller* had been saved by Start Bay fishermen. But there was no way of stopping the lifeboat.

When the *William and Emma*'s crew fought their way close to the wreck of the schooner, they could see that their toil was in vain - the lines hanging from her showed that the

The crew of the William and Emma lifeboat. Only W. Johnson and E. Distin survived.

crew had already been saved. They turned back.

At ten o'clock they reached the Bar. Some of the crew were against trying to cross; the seas over it were worse than when they had set out. But the majority were in favour. They approached and streamed a drogue or sea-anchor and took in all sail except the mizzen. They had started stowing the oars when a massive wave hit the stern of the boat and flung her upwards, at the same time turning her broadside to the waves. The men were flung into the bottom of the boat, but had no time to disentangle themselves before another wave rolled her over. One of the men, Edwin Distin, brother of the cox'n, and one of the only two survivors, hauled himself back to the upside-down boat by the drogue line. A few others of the crew clung to the keel, but were washed off. Most floated away in their lifejackets.

Finally, Edwin Distin and William Johnson were washed ashore under Rickham Common on the eastern side of the Estuary. They had just enough strength to climb on to a rock some 40 yards from the main shore and then could move no more. Finally a thin weighted line was flung to them and then a flask of brandy sent along it. This, and a short rest, gave them enough strength to haul out a stronger rope with lifebuoys attached. Clinging to the buoys, they were pulled to safety. They were reported to have been "so bruised, battered and shocked that they were confined to bed for several weeks".

Some idea of the weather conditions during that time is given by the report that a naval patrol boat attempting to rescue the men got as far as the Blackstone rocks in the teeth of the gale before being forced back, together with other motor boats.

"Eddy" Distin was later appointed coxswain of the replacement lifeboat and volunteers immediately came forward to form the new crew.

Foot Note: Though there are other places in the country which claim Alfred,Lord Tennyson's poem "Crossing the Bar" as referring to their Bar, there seems little doubt that Salcombe Bar was the inspiration for "**Sunset and evening star,**

And one clear call for me!
And may there be no moaning of the bar
When I put out to sea..."

Tennyson visited Salcombe in 1889 and made many trips across the Bar in the yacht *Sunbeam*, on which he lived in the harbour.

The coast path crosses Rickham Common. At its tip you can look down on Limebury Point (earlier called Lambury Point), which is where Distin and Johnson were washed ashore after the lifeboat capsize in 1916. Part of the smashed lifeboat also ended up jammed in between two rocks close to the Point. Lambury Point, the eastern point of the entrance to Salcombe, supplied the stone to build the little pier where the ferries call at the Ferry Inn.

Rickham Common is where the Cromwellian artillery was placed to bombard the Royalists in Fort Charles (Salcombe Castle) from January 15, 1546 until May 8 when the Royalists surrendered. Some earthwork outlines of the artillery emplacements can still be seen on the hillside.

40. PLACIDAS FARROULT.
The Blackstone, 1940.

THIS 136-ton small coaster lies immediately beside the Blackstone inside Lambury Point on the eastern side of the entrance to Salcombe and inside the Bar. The Blackstone stands up 11 feet at low tide and has a beacon on its western side. The ship lies inside and parallel to the rocks on to which she drifted in a south-westerly gale on November 1, 1940.

She was built in France in 1927 and was one of about 20 small French and Belgian ships which escaped at the fall of France in 1940. At this time the Admiralty, fearing invasion, ordered a boom defence to be set up across the entrance to Salcombe Harbour. The *Placidas Farroult* and a French lifeboat were used as gate vessels and all buoys and beacons marking the entrance were removed. The Wolf Buoy, together with some cable, was stored in the hold of the French coaster.

41. ENSIGN
The Blackstone, 1915.

SALCOMBE was usually supplied with coal by sea. The schooner *Ensign* was doing just that when on her way in to Salcombe from Plymouth on January 30, 1915, she failed to tack properly and struck the Blackstone Rock and sank. For some days the 85ft long ship sat there with her topsail showing and it was months before her masts disappeared from sight under the sea (see picture above).

Both gate vessels were securely moored but the *Placidas Farroult* broke free and was badly holed on the Blackstone rocks. She lay on the rocks, her sides corrugated, with her bows to seaward, but the next tide drove her off and she sank broadside on the inside of the Blackstone with her funnel showing at low water. Since then she has settled right into the sand, but for a long time her mast was used as a datum pole for minefields laid locally. The old Wolf Buoy is still in her hold.

42. MEIRION.
Gara Rock, 1879.

IT was a bad run home for the fully-rigged iron barque *Meirion*. And when the 1372-ton ship went ashore in fog on the morning of Sunday October 7, 1879, the stubborn nature of Captain William Williams didn't help to save his ship.

The *Meirion* was just a year old when she left Rangoon on March 19, 1879, laden with 200 tons of rice and 150 tons of the herb called cutch, and headed back to London. She carried a crew of 23 all told.

The first trouble came from a rogue wave which hit them when they were off the Cape of Good Hope. It smashed into the galley area and damaged much of their provisions. Worse, it washed overboard Able Seaman James Taylor and though they turned back they could not find him.

She ran into contrary winds almost all the time. Somewhere on the way she put ashore another of the crew who was suffering from scurvy. When she finally reached the entrance to the English Channel, she ran into fog. Despite their need to get home as soon as possible, Captain Williams made sure that they "felt" their way up to the Lizard, which they sighted when the fog lifted for an hour, and then on the Saturday she also got a sight of the Eddystone. Then the fog clamped down again.

The next time it lifted it was dark, but they could see they were close to land. The wind veered to the south-south-west. Captain Williams tried to tack out of trouble, but missed stays, and the wind blew her on shore at about 2.30 a.m. below Gara Rock Coastguard station.

Normally, Mr. Segrue was in charge at Gara Rock, but he was on leave and it was Mr. Bailey, the commissioned boatman, who got the rocket apparatus into place and with his first shot got a line across the mizzen gaff. Captain Williams ordered the line to be dropped over the stern and told the coastguards: "We don't want that - we want a tug".

The coastguards were considerably miffed by this and told the Captain in no uncertain terms that he was in danger of losing his ship and his crew. But he took no notice, had a boat lowered and with six of his crew set off for Salcombe. On the way he met a coastguard boat coming out from Salcombe to help, but he insisted on going on

The Meirion on shore. The Captain insisted on tugs, but it was too late.

into Salcombe. One of the coastguards transferred to the *Meirion*'s boat to guide them in over the Bar.

Captain Williams could have used either of two steamers in Salcombe at the time to give him a tow, but there seems to have been some confusion and he ended up making arrangements for the tug, *Sir Walter Raleigh*, from Plymouth to come to his aid.

The tug arrived at 2 p.m. By then as Captain Williams had not put down his anchors, both the high tides since he first struck had now carried the *Meirion* further in and on to a more fearsome set of rocks. She was now holed and at dusk the Captain changed his mind about the rocket and breeches buoy and asked for all 21 aboard to be taken ashore.

At high tide on the Monday morning, the *Sir Walter Raleigh* tried to pull her off. But failed. A large steamer going down Channel stood in and sent a boat offering assistance if they would pass a hawser. Captain Williams refused their help. It would probably have done no good. There were now several feet of water inside her and the holes must have been large as the water inside rose and fell with the tide.

The *Meirion* was still there on the Tuesday when Captain Champion and Captain Jones, representing the underwriters, and a Mr.Richard representing the owners, the Avon Shipping Company of Carnarvon, all arrived on the scene. They told the local paper that the ship's value, including her cargo, was £50,000. And they entered into salvage agreements with local firms.

However, soon after the salvage started, her mainmast broke off at deck level and fell bringing down the others. The fall of the masts nearly crushed one of the salvage boats. Only 120 tons of her cargo had been saved when a series of storm stopped the work.

More gales a fortnight later raised enormous seas, which broke her in two. And soon she was completely out of sight.

43. PAULINE
Gara Rock, 1877.

PAULINE died in the night of Sunday, October 14, 1877, but nobody saw what happened. The next morning the coastguards from Rickham Station at Gara Rock found wreckage on the shore, her nameboard, and the eight bodies of her crew on Seccombe and Rickham Sands.

The blame for the tragedy to this French brigantine lies with the severe gale which swung from south to south-west during the storm on that Sunday night. It was found later that the *Pauline* of 200 tons, commanded by Captain B.Nissen was on her way home to Dunkirk from Portugal with a cargo of figs, nuts and cork.

At the inquest on the bodies, Charles Harris, Chief Officer of Rickham coastguards, said that he was told at 4 a.m. on the Monday morning that the remains of a ship were on Rickham Sands, close to his station. No one on watch during the night had seen lights or anything to tell them a ship was in trouble. Other witnesses at the inquest thought that from the position of the wreckage the ship had been picked up by a huge wave, washed on to the rocks and then broke to pieces as the wave receded. They also felt, from the fact that the bodies were not much disfigured and that they were washed up on Seccombe and Rickham Sands, that the crew had been washed off the ship before she struck.

Foot Note: The Gara Rock Hotel was originally built in 1842 as the Rickham Coastguard Station. After the sale of the station in 1909 it became a family boarding house and then the hotel.

Gara Rock has been called Gatter Rock, Gata, Garter and Gaytor, but all are derived from the Saxon word for "settlement".

The grave of the crew of the *Pauline* was close to the belfrey door of East Portlemouth Church, but the headstone was removed recently to make more space in this crowded graveyard. In East Portlemouth churchyard is the grave of 77-year-old Richard Jarvis, whose murderess, his servant girl, was the last person ever burned at the stake for the crime of poisoning in 1782. They do say, however, that she was executed by hanging before being burned in Exeter.

44. BRONZE SWORD WRECK.
Moor Sand, 1000BC.

Phil Baker with the Bronze Age sword he discovered while teaching novices to dive off Moor Sand.

SWORDS and axe-heads made of bronze marked the underwater grave of a tin trader of ancient days in Moor Sand bay. On shore a large noticeboard warns everyone to keep away as that the tin trader's grave is today a protected wreck.

This protection was given in 1978 after diving instructor Phil Baker, while teaching beginners in the shallows, found a fine bronze sword and two other bronze weapons on the seabed there. In 1978 an archaeological survey was carried out under the direction of the late Keith Muckelroy and more 3,000-year-old bronze weapons including two axe-heads, were discovered. But no other traces of a wreck were found, just eight Middle Bronze Age weapons. These finds would appear to tie in with the Erme Mouth discoveries (see Wreck No.2) and might explain what a Bronze Age ship was doing here.

Foot Note: Moor Sand is the bay just to the west of the headland known as Pig's Nose. It is interesting to note the old time fishermen's "baconian" obsession when naming rocks and headlands in the area - we have the Pig's Nose, the Ham Stone (another one, but not so grand as the one off the Bolt), and Gammon Head!

The big notice-board warning that Moor Sand is a protected wreck site is mounted on the cliff so that it can be clearly seen from the sea by diving boats.

45. RELIANCE.
Gammon Head, 1888.

THIS 31-ton paddlesteamer tug foundered on December 30, 1888, in a Force Six north-easterly. The 98ft-long tug was under tow by another tug, the *Conqueror* and was bound from Gravesend, Kent, to Troon, Scotland, when she sprang a leak and was abandoned by her crew of four. She was built at Yarmouth in 1874. She is in a gully 60 feet down just off Gammon Head. Divers say that two big boilers and paddles are to be seen as well as the engine, iron frames and wooden planking.

The paddlesteamer tug Reliance at work near Gravesend in the 1880s. The big sailing ship getting ready for a tow is the Collingwood, built in 1872

THE PIRATE GOLD OF GARA ROCK

THERE are reports of gold and silver coins being found on the beaches under the cliffs all along the coast from Gara Rock to Prawle Point and particularly around Gammon Head. Any sailing ship caught on these lee shores in a South-Westerly gale, stood little chance of escape from those great cliffs or the rock claws at their feet.

It is not surprising therefore to read of coins being washed up on beaches. One newspaper of the late 1800s records the even older oral tradition of lost treasure ships by writing: "Just inside Gammon Head two Spanish galleons went ashore. Doubloons were being picked up there after two centuries." Of course, you have to take such reports with a little salt - every lost ship was a Spanish galleon and every coin a "doubloon".

In olden days too, every foreign ship was liable to be called a "Barbary pirate". It is said that no merchant ship of the 1600s was safe in the waters off the South Devon coast. However, it is true that Barbary pirates did hunt up and down the whole of the English Channel. In one particular year these pirates from the Barbary Coast ports of northwest Africa are recorded as capturing six ships out of Dartmouth, making slaves of their crews and offering their captains for ransom. In 1641 there were 25,000 Christian slaves in Algiers alone and all taken from European ships.

However, in 1996 a group of divers in the water a quarter of a mile offshore between the Gara Rock Hotel and the Bronze Age site of Moor Sand (see Wreck No.44) made a discovery which proved that you should never discount old stories of lost pirate ships or tales of the treasure they carried.

One of those divers, Ron Howell of Totnes, working to establish an archaeological survey of a group of four cannon, which had been found earlier, tells of diving on a day when it was near freezing in the boat and no better in the water. Complete with measuring tape and a clipboard for recording such details, Ron sank reluctantly down the shot line into the 20m-deep gloom around the cannon.

Only at his third attempt to tie the measuring tape firmly to the cascabel of one of the cannon did he suceed. His efforts had let water into his mask. As he tilted his head back to clear it and vision returned, something glittered close to him in the wall of the gully.

His forefinger probed into a crack. A moment later and he was staring at a gleaming gold coin. Small, but definitely gold! Then, as he looked closely at the rocks around him, he could see another golden spot. And another.

The face and reverse of just one of the 600 coins - in perfect condition despite having been more than 360 years under the sea.

IT'S TIRING WORK BRINGING UP GOLD COINS FROM DEEP UNDER THE SEA!

Divers (left to right):
Neville Oldham, Mick Kightley, Ron Howell, Mick Palmer; (foreground) Dave Illingworth, Mike Evans.
The coastal footpath to Gara Rock runs along the cliffs in the background.

When his air ran out and he made a near free ascent back to the rigid-hulled inflatable boat, bucking in the swell over the cannon, he had four coins so tightly gripped in one hand that their imprint was not to fade from his flesh for some time!

He managed to get aboard without opening his clenched fist. When he did, a boatload of divers of the South-West Maritime Archaeological Group, who had earlier been extremely reluctant to dive, all seemed to leave the boat in five seconds flat! However, this severe attack of gold fever was soon over. By the next dive archaeological discipline was restored!

Those four coins were the start of a huge treasure find, the first of over 600 gold coins, gold jewellery, and little gold ingots to be raised from this wreck and carried into Salcombe. Today they are valued by experts at thousands and thousands of pounds.

They were not easily raised. It took over two years, 3,800 dives and almost as many hours underwater for 13 divers to tease the coins from the cracks in the rocks or to fan the

PART OF A PIRATE'S SHARE?

Nearly all the jewellery had been cut up as though it was valued for its weight not looks.

GOLDFINGER

Were these two fine creations intended to end up like this gold finger ingot?

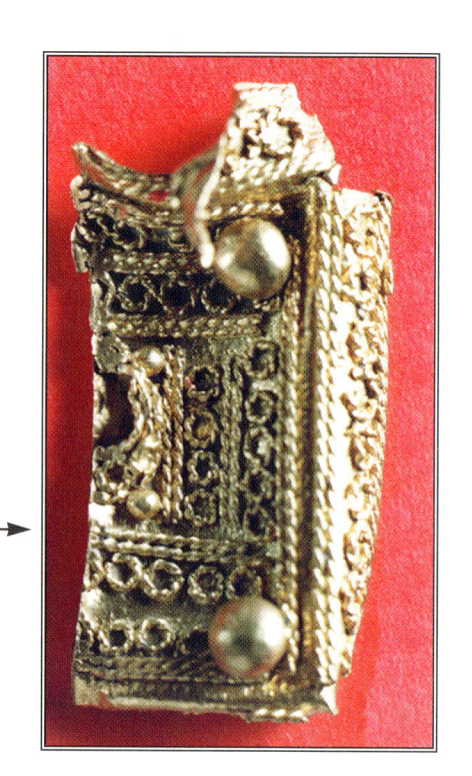

sand off more gold on the floor of the gullies. It was always cold work and often so dark that the divers had to use torches.

But it was diving time well spent for British Museum coin experts say this is the finest "assemblage" of such gold coins ever found in Europe.

First dives to survey the cannon site were made by Mick Palmer of Northampton, local archaeologist-divers Neville Oldham and Stephen George, and Staffordshire divers Mike Williams and his wife Julie.

They soon found that there were few obvious signs of a wreck apart from more iron cannon spread out in other shallow gullies. There are, in fact, 11 heavily-encrusted cannon in all. Most of the guns are seven-footers with the longest 8ft 6in. Two are small swivel guns. Two ancient anchors lie nearby.

Many of the team who have worked this cannon and treasure site had been fully occupied further to the west only a year earlier on a sensational discovery in the mouth of the River Erme - the wreck of a Bronze Age ship and her cargo of crudely-shaped ingots of pure tin (See Wreck No.2). What little diving time they had to spare was spent on a survey of another famous West Country shipwreck - that of the *Gossamer*, a fully-rigged China tea clipper wrecked in a gale in December 1868 near Prawle Point (See Wreck No 57). The only time those archaeological divers would move away from these important sites was when they were blown off by south-easterly winds. Then they would head for the cannon site and work on the pre-disturbance survey. It was on one of these "blown-off" days that they made the first gold strike.

The divers are known as "The South-West Maritime Archaelogical Group" As diving advisers they have Mike Kingston and Mick Kightley, of Northampton, and Neville Oldham, of nearby Stoke Fleming. The other members are Mick Palmer, Andy Elliott, Dave Dunkley, Richard Boon and Mike Evans of Northampton, Jim Tyson, of Market Harborough, Mike Williams of Staffordshire, Stephen George of Slapton, Ron Howell of Totnes, and Dave Illingworth of Hope Cove.

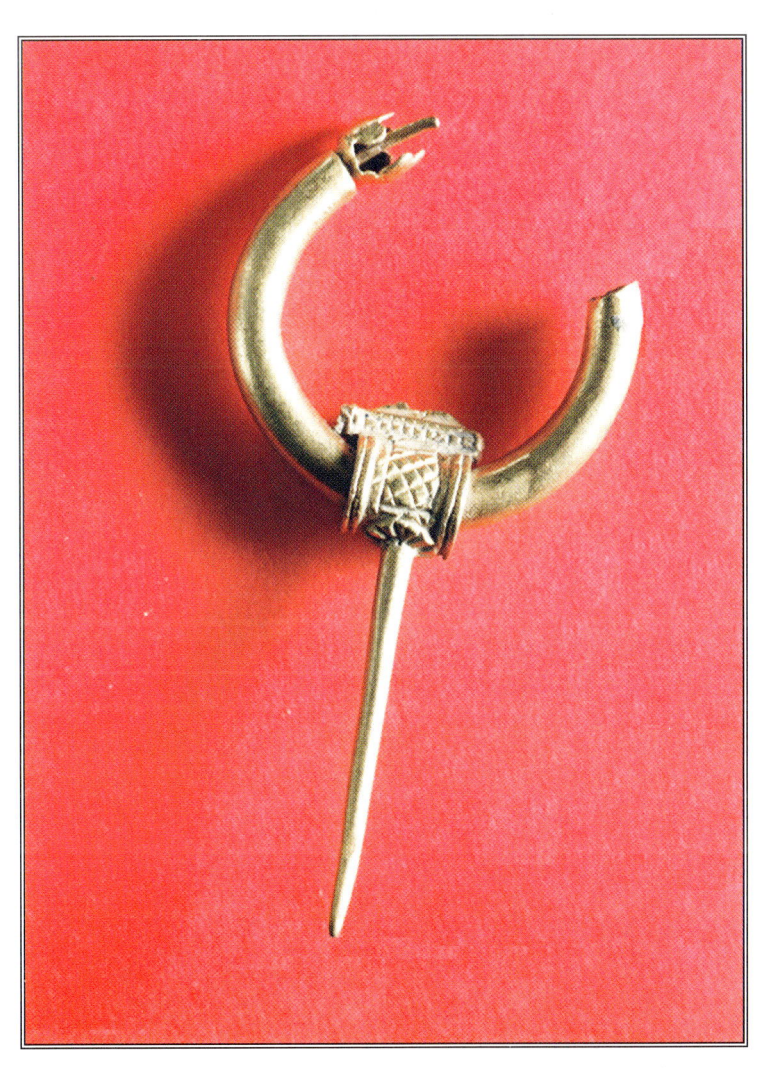

All their diving has produced other artifacts as well as the coins, jewellery and ingots - long pewter spoons of Elizabethan times; an unusual sounding lead in the shape of a fish; a roll of lead; a Bellarmine jar or rather part of it; German pottery; a brass seal with the initials M and R entwined under a diamond shape. And the same initials but the other way round on the base of a pewter bowl, which is six inches across and stands three inches high. The divers thought the initials were bound to identify the ship or at least the seal's owner. But despite intensive research they have no clue so far to the ship's name.

Among the artifacts is an apothecary's jar which is believed to have come originally from Somerset. Seeds found close by, turned out to be broad beans of the 17th century. Experts at Kew Gardens say that they are genetically 85 per cent akin to the broad beans we grow in our gardens today. Broad beans in oil were a delicacy in the Middle East of those days, but they were also used as a diuretic, which might place them in the ship's doctor's medicine chest.

What makes the Moroccan coins the divers found so valuable is their rarity. They are quarter dinars, half dinars and dinars from Morocco, dating from 520AD to 1632. They bear the name of various sheikhs and represent four dynasties. In the whole of their national collections, Britain has only six similar pieces, the French have 12 and Morocco won't say, but it is believed to have very few.

The vast majority of the coins date from the late 1500s to 1632. They come from the period when European ships suffered most from the attacks of Barbary pirates, who emerged from the Mediterranean and attacked English shipping around Plymouth and Dartmouth in search of loot and slaves. Was this one of those Barbary pirate ships? Or was she a British privateer homeward bound for Salcombe with a share of the loot taken away from those same pirates?

Though the ship may never be named, the fact that the gold coins recovered by the divers cover such a long period and

Happy divers after a "gold rush".
Left to right: Mick Palmer, Mick Kightley, Ron Howell, Jim Tyson and Andy Elliott.

DO YOU KNOW THESE INITIALS?

The divers believe that this seal, belonging to the Captain, or someone important aboard, will help them solve the mystery of the pirate gold.

also that the gold jewellery - earrings, torques, brooches and bracelets - is without any precious stones in the settings and is often cut, almost chopped into pieces, suggests that this is a Barbary pirate's share of loot, more important for the weight of the gold than its looks.

The vandalism of the jewellery is made worse by the harm done to the artistic work which went into its original creation. One of the pieces, now slashed in two and minus the fine stone which would have been its centrepiece, is almost identical to a brooch hanging from the neck of Mary, Queen of Scots, in a famous portrait of her with James I when he was six. (See page v, top left).

The discovery of the ingots suggests that other jewellery had already been melted down. The shape of the gold "finger" ingots is explained by their name. A scrape was made in earth with a finger and then molten gold was poured into the depression.

Almost as incredible as its discovery is the fact that the secret of the gold find was kept for more than two whole years. All was revealed, however, when a press conference was held by the divers, the British Museum and the Receiver of Wreck, shortly after the Government listing of the site as that of a protected historic wreck at 50 12.69N; 03 44.679W.

Today if you look down and out to the east from the Gara Rock Hotel and the former coastguard lookout there, you will often see a diving boat anchored over the wreck. That is because the authorised search for a clue to the ship's identity and more of her cargo of treasure still goes on.

The Lalla Rookh pictured in Surrey Commercial Dock, London. Her crew were some of the first men to be rescued by rocket apparatus.

46. LALLA ROOKH.
Elender Cove, 1873.

THIS beautiful square-rigged tea clipper took her name from the even more beautiful daughter of the Emperor of Delhi, who, according to the poems of Thomas Moore, was beguiled by a handsome Persian poet while on her way to her arranged marriage with the Sultan of Cashmere. Lalla Rookh fell in love with the poet but had to leave him and go on dutifully to the marriage to the sultan, whom she had never seen. But, surprise, surprise, the poet turns out to have been the sultan in disguise.... Say "Aaah"!

Unfortunately the ship named after the princess did not have such a happy ending. She was wrecked when homeward bound from Shanghai for London with a cargo of 1300 tons of tea and ten tons of tobacco, valued at over £100,000. In command was Captain George Fullerton with 18 crew, one passenger and a stowaway aboard.

She left Shanghai on the 22nd of October,1872 and during the last part of her voyage had such favourable winds that she ran 3,000 miles in a fortnight. She passed the Lizard on Sunday March 2 at 10 p.m and steered east-south-east, a course which should certainly have taken her clear of Prawle and Start Points. Later Captain Fullerton said that he thought the compass must have been misread.

Whatever the reason, there is no doubt that on Monday, March 3, 1873, at 5.45 a.m. in dense fog,the 869-ton *Lalla Rookh* in full sail before a south-westerly gale, struck Gammon Head, about half a mile to the west of Prawle Point. George Fullerton dropped both his anchors and for a moment they held, but the next sea lifted her and wrenched out her anchors. She was then adrift, but was carried on round into Elender Cove, a sandy little bay under high cliffs. Here one of her masts collapsed, and, in doing so, pushed out some of her bottom plates and she started to sink.

By then she had four fewer crew aboard, as they had been in the bow and had jumped on to the rocks at Gammon Head when she first struck. Another 15 people were saved by breeches buoy when a rocket line was put across her at the first attempt by Prawle Coastguards.

The only casualties were the Mate, Thomas Groves, who was drowned when he and four seamen launched a boat which capsized, and the stowaway, who, it is believed, was dead in his bunk from dysentery, before the ship was wrecked. Within a week the ship broke in two, but not before 100 cases of tea had been salvaged as well as many of the ship's fittings.

The ship is interesting for two other reasons. One is that her figurehead was picked up on a beach in Jersey – and can now be seen on board the *Cutty Sark* at Greenwich, London. And the second is that this was one of the first ships to have her crew rescued by the newfangled rocket apparatus.

In RNLI records a description of the rescue from the *Lalla Rookh*, shows just how new this method was then: **"It was just becoming light when she struck a rock and this was seen by one of the coastguards. He whistled to warn the crew of their danger, but seeing it was in vain, ran to the station for the rocket apparatus.**

"Mr Segrue (the Chief Boatman) and his men speedily got it, brought it to the scene of the disaster, where it was worked with a will. The first line fell across the ship and was secured. The basket soon followed. One man and a boy went across singly, but the rest of the crew, who clustered on the mizzen top-mast, most of them nearly naked, hesitated to trust themselves to the basket two at a time until Captain Fullerton, the master, said that he would set an example and got in with sailor. When they were drawn ashore there was no longer any hesitation and the men followed, the coastguards working the apparatus with such hearty good will that in 25 minutes the fifteen were rescued..."

Foot Note:The remains of the *Lalla Rookh* are completely scattered around in shallow water in the cove.

47. GLAD TIDINGS.
Elender Cove, 1882.

A 1292-ton fully-rigged Canadian sailing ship carrying a cargo of linseed oil from Calcutta and bound for Amsterdam, the *Glad Tidings* ran on to rocks in thick fog on December 15, 1882.

This came as more of a shock to Captain Charles McMullan than anyone else as he was below at the time she struck. He was consulting his charts and had just convinced himself that he was nearly six miles offshore! The mate did try to get her to go about when he saw the land ahead, but it was too late for her to complete her turn and she struck stern first a quarter of a mile north-west of Prawle Point and almost into Elender Cove. She was so close to the cliffs that they cut away her mizzen mast to enable them to get along it to shore.

However, before they could use the mast as their escape route, one of the crew, lighting distress signals, let sparks fall into the lazarette hatch where paint was stored and soon the whole ship was ablaze.

Fortunately, the Rickham coastguard team with rocket apparatus reached them in time to save 19 of her crew. Two others drowned when trying to swim ashore.

48. MARIA.
Langler Rocks, 1892.

On June 27, 1892, the Greek steamer *Maria* ran on to Langler Rocks, on the west side of Prawle Point in thick fog. The Salcombe lifeboat went to help, but by the time they reached the ship the two passengers and 23 crew had rowed ashore in their own boat. The *Maria* had a short life. She was launched in Sunderland in May, 1891 and was declared a total wreck on July 19, 1892.

49. IDA.
Prawle Point, 1930.

Whether the fright they were given when another steamer suddenly burst out of the fog almost on top of them at 9.30 p.m. on Monday, September 22, 1930, had anything to do with it - as the Master claimed - or whether they were simply lost in that fog, the fact is that the *Ida* ran at half speed on to the rocks just to the west of Prawle Point half an hour later.

The *Ida* was a single-propellor, single funnel Belgian steamer of 504 tons, which had been loaded with 580 tons of coal at Cardiff and was heading for Portsmouth. The steamer was built in 1920 and was first called *Pembrey* when

When the fog cleared, the Ida's crew found themselves aground under Prawle Point

owned by an Anglesey company, who later sold her to the Societe Belge D'Armaments Maritime.

She plunged into the dense fog which blanketed the whole of the Channel almost as soon as she rounded Land's End and stayed in that murk until she ran aground. The identity of the steamer with which she had so nearly collided in the fog just a short while before was never discovered.

However, despite the fog, the men manning the signal station on Prawle could see her flares and hear the crew's shouts coming from an area almost directly beneath them. They alerted the coastguards, who set the whole rescue operation into action. Both Plymouth and Torbay lifeboats were called out, as well as the Prawle rocket rescue team. Some of the Prawle men climbed down the cliffs to the rocks and there found that one of the crew of the *Ida* had swum nearly all the way ashore with a line tied round his waist. The Prawle men jumped into the water and helped him in as the waves breaking on the rocks looked likely to smash the exhausted man to pieces.

Though this line was useful, it was not going to be of much help compared with the steel hawser used to ferry men ashore in the breeches buoy. So the rocket team dropped another line neatly over the steamer with their first attempt and, with the coastguards and villagers from East Prawle hauling, the other eleven of the crew were soon hoisted safely to the top of the 150ft cliffs by breeches buoy.

During this time the Plymouth lifeboat was searching in the fog for the wreck, but finally had to give up, and went back without having seen any sign of her. The Torbay lifeboat did better arriving at midnight, but though her services were not required she stood by with a tug waiting for it to get light.

Soon after dawn, the fog lifted and the 165-foot-long *Ida* could be seen, close in and just to the west of the Point. She was listing to starboard. The sea was then so calm that three men of the crew swam out to her to collect their belongings. When they returned they reported that she was making water and was totally surrounded by rocks. Two tugs came out to her, but could not see how to move her, and forecast that she was going to be a total wreck. They were right. Two weeks later a gale and big seas broke her in two. And shortly after that she disappeared completely from sight.

50. BONA.
Prawle Point, 1907.

DENSE fog in the Channel in the early hours of Sunday, August 4, 1907, was the cause of the loss of the sailing ship *Bona*. Her captain Charles Haste could hardly blame the state of the sea for the wreck. It was almost flat calm with little more than a light breeze ruffling the surface.

The Bona, an 80-ton ketch was loaded with good Welsh coal at Llanelli, which she was due to carry to Mistley, up the River Stour from Harwich.

With the wind behind her and all sails set, she ran ashore at 12.15 a.m.in the rock gullies just to the west of Prawle Point. She was so close to the coastguard station that the watch could hear shouts for help from almost right below them. The coastguards telephoned for Salcombe lifeboat and she was launched at once. When the lifeboat crew got to the scene they found the *Bona* underwater with the sea reaching half-way up her mainsail. There was no sign of the crew.

When the lifeboat got back to Salcombe at six in the morning after searching the area for the missing crew, they were told that Prawle coastguards had telephoned again to say that they had picked up a empty lifeboat marked "Bona, Ipswich", but there was still no news of the crew. Shortly after that another message stopped them worrying - the crew of four had rowed and sailed all the way to Dartmouth in another small boat and had landed there "partially clothed", but unhurt.

The next day the *Bona* slid off the rocks, dumping her cargo just 30 yards off to the west of the Point, but she was still awash. The Dartmouth tugs *Victor* and *Venture* came to try and tow her to Dartmouth, but managed to pull her only a hundred yards before she sank from sight in much deeper water. This time she stayed there. Her steering wheel floated into Salcombe Harbour two days later.

51. LOUISE YVONNE.
Prawle Island. 1935.

The end of an onion seller's supplier. The Louise Yvonne ashore at Prawle Island.

FRENCH onion sellers, who used to push their bicycles from house to house in every big town in England between the wars (and after the Second World War, though the trade seems to have died out now) had to have a good supply of those strings of onions to hang from their handlebars.

The *Louise Yvonne* which ran into Prawle Point on September 29, 1935, was one of the motor vessels which made sure that those bicycles were well stocked. This two-masted boat actually ran in between Prawle Island and Gull Rock.

This all took place in dense fog and at three o'clock in the morning, but because it was half-tide she got so far in that the three crew, the captain and the captain's two daughters in their early twenties, who were also aboard (Louise and Yvonne?) were able to step on shore. They stayed in East Prawle village for some time after the wreck, but left after all attempts by a tug failed to pull her off. The Captain's two young daughters were reported in the Kingsbridge Gazette as "little the worse for their alarming experience" but the captain was "considerably upset by the plight of his vessel and in halting English said he was sick and tired".

Foot Note: For a long time the bows of the onion boat showed above water right underneath the coastguard station, but the arrival of yet another wreck changed all that (see Wreck No.52).

52. HEYE-P.
Prawle Island, 1979.

This 296-ton West German motor vessel was carrying a cargo of china clay from Par to Velsen, Holland, when, after engine trouble, near-hurricane winds flung her aground on Prawle Island on December 16, 1979. The 155ft-long *Heye-P* broke her back almost immediately.

The Salcombe lifeboat, *Baltic Exchange*, was quickly on the scene but the seas were too big - breaking right over the wreck - for her to get close enough to take off the three-

The Heye-P was flung ashore on Prawle Island. Her crew were rescued by helicopter. Picture: South Hams Newspapers.

man crew. That rescue was carried out by a helicopter from HMS Culdrose, the R.N. Air Station on the Lizard, Cornwall. But it would have been impossible without the Prawle Coastguards, who brought portable searchlights to the scene.

The rescue reports give some idea of the conditions. One says that the helicopter pilot was blinded by sheets of spray even though he was hovering high above the wreck while winching up the crew.

Foot Note: Part of her stern wreckage dries at low water and can be seen between Gull Island and Prawle Island. Her wreckage lies across that of the *De Boot* (see Wreck No.55) and *HMS Crocodile* (see Wreck No.53), and right on top of the *Louise Yvonne* (see Wreck No.51), whose wreckage was pushed right under the new arrival.

53. H.M.S. CROCODILE.
Prawle Island, 1784.

THEY beat Patrick Crawley to death in an orderly manner for what he did after *HMS Crocodile* hit "the Praule" in the deep dark before dawn on May 9, 1784.

In truth Ordinary Seaman Crawley would have been better off if he had died in the sinking of that 24-gun frigate belonging to His Majesty George the Third, but like all the rest of the crew he survived the actual wreck, only to become the ship's only casualty for what he did, in drink, at the wreck site on Prawle Point.

It wasn't until months after the wreck that Patrick Crawley's final agony began. Early one morning in autumn a yellow flag broke out from the topmasthead of *HMS Princess Royal*. As the flag fluttered in the first of the wind a solitary gun boomed out across Portsmouth harbour.

Ten ships of the Fleet lay in the anchorage and the single gunshot was the signal that punishment was about to begin. It was also the signal to muster each ship's crew upon her deck to witness that punishment. Only the chronic sick were excused. For though the Admiralty was not particularly concerned about the punishment of poor Patrick, nor in his death by the cat o' nine tails, they were concerned to make sure that all the 8,000 men in those ten ships saw what would happen to them if they breached the discipline which ruled their daily lives.

Crawley had struck a superior officer and that could not be allowed. He must be seen to pay for such a crime.

Even from the ships furthest away from the flagship, *Princess Royal*, the red coats of the Marines could be seen as they climbed down into the punishment boat. With them went the drummer, his drum muffled in a piece of black cloth. Then they brought Crawley down. If he stumbled it was not from fear, but the vast quantity of rum that comrades had smuggled to him to muffle his pain. With Crawley was the Bosun's Mate of the *Princess Royal*. And bright as a Marine's jacket was the red baize of the bag he carried down to the boat with him.

"One hundred lashes with a Cat of Nine Tails on his bare back alongside such ships as were in Portsmouth Harbour at the time".

That had been Crawley's sentence at the court-martial held on June 7 that year in the great stern cabin of the same man o' war from which he now stepped into the punishment boat. Without any delay he was strung up to a tall triangle of wood set up just aft of the oarsmen. His sentence was read aloud and then a nod from the Princess Royal's captain ordered the punishment to begin. The Bosun's Mate opened the red bag...

The punishment was to be divided equally between the ten ships. So Patrick Crawley took the first ten on his bare back at the flagship's side and then with the drum sounding the muffled slow beat of the "Rogue's March", the boat, with Crawley still strung up, was rowed over to the next ship.

The next ten lashes were given by the bosun's mate of that ship. And unless he gave them with all his strength, he too could find himself facing a taste of the Cat. And so, from ship to ship, the punishment went on. Only the surgeon in the boat could stop it and then, unless Crawley was already dead, it would only be punishment delayed until he was able to take the rest. Naval records detail that

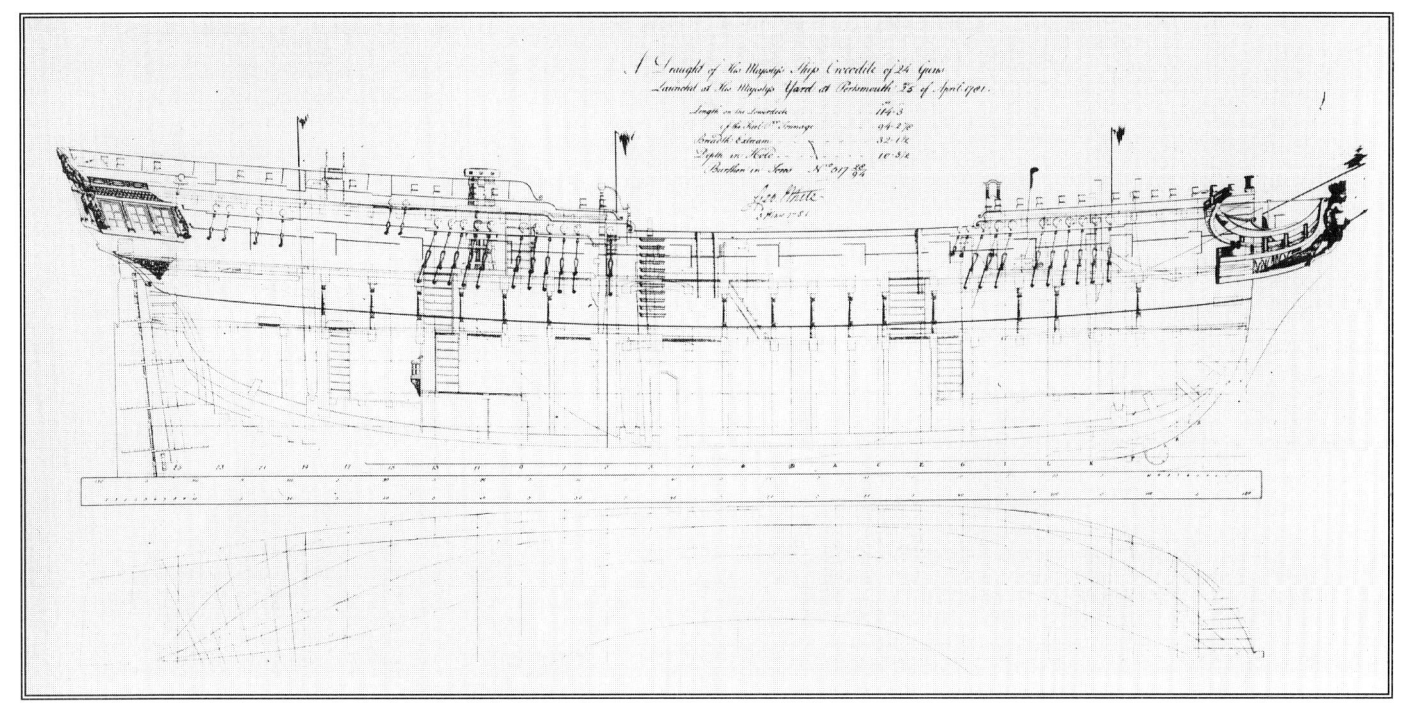

The builder's drawing shows how small HMS Crocodile really was - 170 men were crammed into 114 feet 3 inches.

some men died after 50 lashes. Others took 200 and lived. One man survived after having borne 600 at the rate of 200 every fortnight. It is just possible that Crawley survived. The Navy merely records that the punishment was carried out and does not note if he lived or died.

Crawley's crime took place when all the *Crocodile*'s crew were safe ashore in the village of East Prawle, a short distance inland from the site of the wreck.

The events which led up to it, and turned East Prawle into a home for drunken sailors, began, as far as Patrick Crawley was concerned when he sailed aboard *HMS Crocodile* for Bengal and Madras in the summer of 1783. Patrick Crawley was a volunteer, not a pressed man, one of 170 men crammed into the 114 feet of the frigate's length. As soon as the *Crocodile* arrived in India she was given despatches to carry home to England. She left Madras and sailed round India to Bombay, arriving there on the day after Christmas. More despatches and she was off again. After rounding Africa, she reached St.Helena on March 24, 1784, left there the next day and at 10.15 in the morning of May 8, Captain John Williamson, her commander, sighted the Scillies.

Now with the wind behind her and England, home and beauties dead ahead, the *Crocodile* romped up the Channel at her top speed of 14 knots and headed for Portsmouth. Despite his desire to get home the speed did not please her captain. He thought it too fast for the conditions. The ship was now running into small banks of fog.

So, despite the fact that he usually had every confidence in the ship's Master, Charles Roberts, who had taken the *Crocodile* safely to India and back, on this occasion he overruled him and ordered some sails to be taken in and their course altered further to the south. Both the Captain and Roberts now agreed that they were well out into mid-Channel and out of trouble.

It therefore came as a great shock - which was felt throughout the ship - when at half past two in the morning of May 9, 1784, *HMS Crocodile* ran straight into the west side of Prawle Point.

They were now in a blanket of thick fog. They couldn't see where they were, nor even the shore. But there was no doubt that they were firmly aground and close in, because when Captain Williamson, who had come on deck immediately after the shock had woken him, looked over the ship's port side, he could see "the wash of the sea from the rocks".

They tried, of course, to get her off. It was calm enough, though there was some swell. They launched a boat and sounded around her and then they carried out two kedge anchors, one directly astern and the other to starboard. They winched as hard as they could but still she wouldn't budge. Worse news came from the ship's carpenter - she was holed and the water was rising inside her. So they cut away the masts and threw over anything which would lighten ship, but it was all to no avail. The tide started to ebb, but the ship was clearly lost. Captain Williamson put all his precious despatches into a boat and ordered it ashore. Minutes later as the fog lifted and they could see Prawle Point looming over them, the *Crocodile* toppled over on to her port side. But every man, including Patrick Crawley, got ashore without harm.

The news of her loss spread swiftly. Lloyds List of Tuesday, May 11, 1784, reported: "The Crocodile, Man of War, from Bombay, is lost off the Start". This seems sufficient to have caused an error to be repeated again and again over the years with someone soon adding for good measure "200 men lost", apparently because that was her full complement. The fact that the *Crocodile* was lost at Prawle with no casualties seems to have escaped general notice.

All 170 of the crew - Captain Williamson complained at his own court-martial for losing his ship that he was "thirty men short of complement" - were safe and sound and free of the ship. They were on dry land with space to spare after months cramped up in the frigate. It is difficult to imagine the effect this had on the men. It is even more difficult to imagine the effect it had on East Prawle. Into this small cluster of houses and barns swept sailors without belongings, just a few clothes to cover parts of their tanned nakedness. Sailors suddenly free from the violent discipline of their small ship.

Well, not entirely free. Captain Williamson might have lost his ship, but he wasn't going to let her go without salvaging everything possible. He first commandeered a barn for his men to sleep in. This was considered a great act of charity on his part, but in fact it kept the men together as though they were still in a ship. And so there was no misunderstanding that they were still in the Royal Navy, he mustered the whole ship's company and read the Articles of War to them. This chilling recital of punishments for anyone who "ran" or deserted - death - for anyone who disobeyed an order - death - for anyone who struck a superior officer - the cat - who was drunk - the cat - should have damped down the men's high spirits, but it seems that they went about the work of salvage at each low water in a very light-hearted way. As for drunkeness...without money and in a little village? Impossible you might think, but in that case you don't know what sailors are. Or how quickly a villager could spot an opportunity.

The *Crocodile* crewmen got drink from somewhere. So much that it was impossible to get some of them sober enough to row out to the wreck. This is where Charles Roberts, the Master, ran into trouble. Seeing William Smith, a bosun's mate, dodging away from a work detail, Roberts went after him and grabbed him by the arm. Smith reacted violently, smiting the Master such a blow with his fist that it knocked him unconscious to the ground. After just a glance at the Master's sprawled figure, and knowing there would be no mercy for what he had done, drink or no drink, Smith took to his heels. He had struck a superior officer. Smith was lucky. At the court-martial later, it was said that "he has not since been met with".

Crawley was not to be so fortunate. There was a house in East Prawle, where one or two of the senior non-commissioned officers had found lodgings. It was also a house,"not a publick house", said Mr.William Cockran, the master's mate who lodged there, "but a house where they sold liquor". Crawley came there on the second day after the wreck. And at just the wrong time. He had obviously already found some booze, probably local cider, and he reeled into the house shouting for "grog". Just arrived at the house to have supper with William Cockran, was Mr. John Burn, a petty officer of the *Crocodile*. Burn, who was described as "a man of warm temper", took exception to this drunken sailor yelling for grog just when he was looking forward to his meal. He ordered Crawley out.

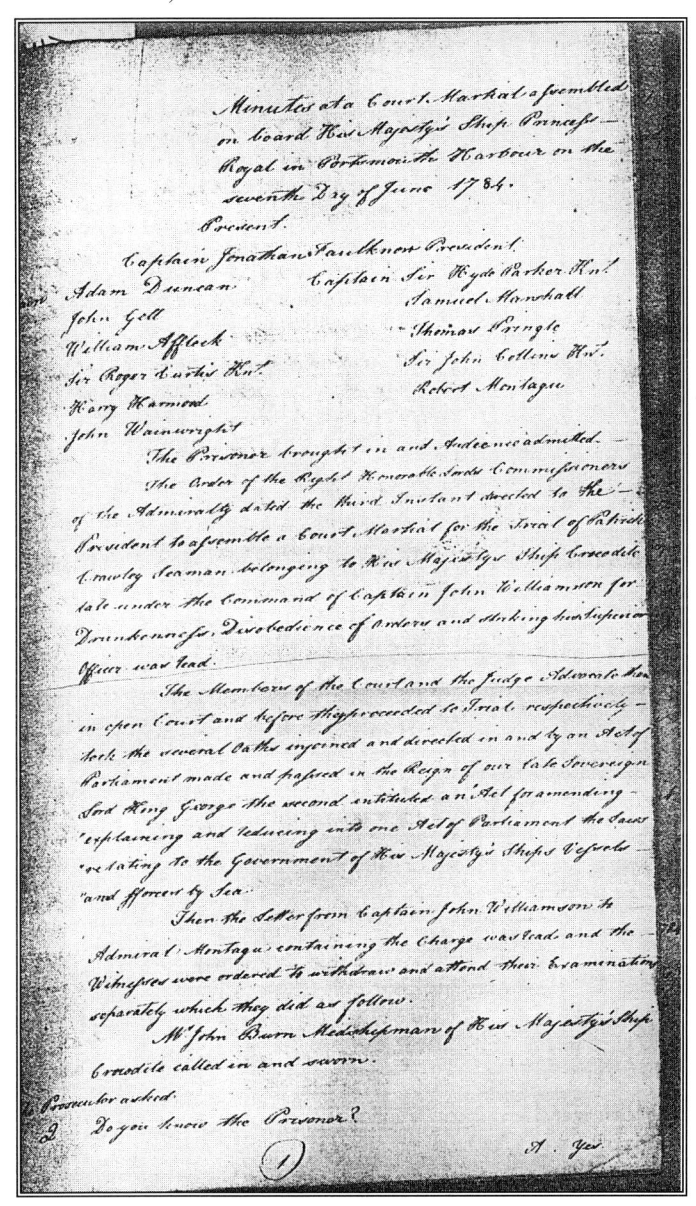

When Crawley went on shouting for drink, Burn took him by the arm and pushed him roughly towards the door. Crawley pushed back. In the following scuffle, Crawley aimed a blow at Burn which would have hit him in the face if it hadn't been so weak that Burn easily warded it off, and ejected Crawley from the house. Burn reported the blow. A court-martial followed automatically.

At this trial, John Burn appears to have tried to be fair when questioned by Captain Williamson:

"When I ordered you and the Officer to take the People down to the shore to go off and save what stores they could, did you ever order him upon that service and did he obey it?"

"I ordered him once and he went on board."

"Are you sure he went on board?"

"I saw him on board."

"Did you see the Prisoner at any other time drunk, but at the time specified?"

"I did not."

The President of the Court, Captain Jonathan Faulknor, then intervened with a few questions of his own:

"Was it a private house that the Prisoner came for liquor?"

"The People of the house, I believe, sold liquor next door."

"In what manner did the Prisoner strike you?"

"He struck at me with his clenched hand. I avoided the

blow by putting up my arm."

"Do you think the Prisoner was sensible enough to know you were his Officer at the time when he struck you?"

"Yes, he mentioned my name."

"Do you mean to say that the Prisoner did strike you, or that he would have struck you had you not warded off the blow?"

"He certainly would have struck had I not guarded the blow off."

Captain Faulknor tried one last question: "Is the Prisoner subject to insanity or is he deemed to be mad at times?"

"Not that I ever heard," said Burn, and Crawley's fate was sealed. Only insanity would justify the striking of a senior officer in Captain Faulknor's book and probably all the other eleven captains hearing the case felt the same way.

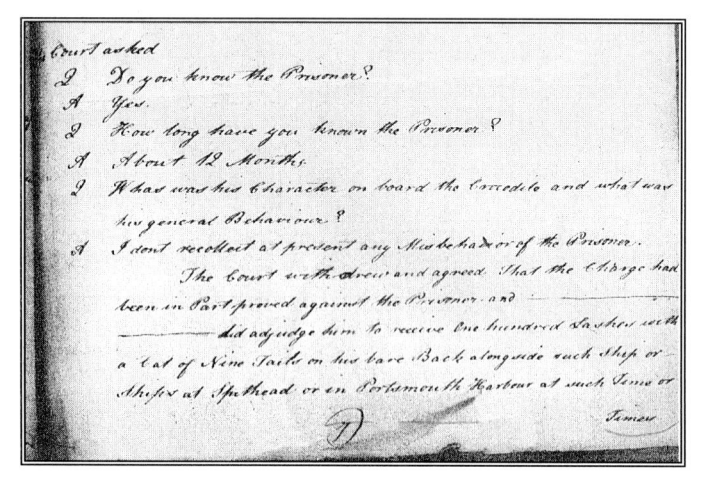

Other witnesses testified to Crawley's good character. It was clear that Crawley was so drunk at the time he did not know what he was doing. William Cockran, the master's mate, testified that on the morning after Crawley had come to their lodgings "took off his hat and offered to make any concession to Mr.Burn for striking him as he was insensible at the time and knew nothing of it, but that his shipmates had informed him that he had used Mr.Burn ill."

At the end of the court-martial Patrick Crawley had his say. It was very simple: "I was on board and did my duty as well as any man in the ship from the time we were cast away."

When the captains returned after considering their verdict, they had decided that the charge was "part proved", which seemed a way of saying that John Burn's "warm temper" was also partly to blame. Perhaps they were being kind, or thought they were, when they gave him only 100 lashes instead of the 300-500 normally given as punishment for anyone charged as he was with "drunkenness, disobedience of orders, and striking his superior officer". Crawley was put in irons in the *Princess Royal* to await punishment, while back at the Prawle the work of salvage went on.

Proper salvage had started very quickly after the wreck, which now lay on its port side between Prawle Island, which is really a big rock, slightly to the west of and almost attached to Prawle Point, and the sea-level arch in the tip of the 300ft high Point itself. Letters to Mark Milbank, Esq., Vice-Admiral of the Blue and Commander in Chief of His Majesty's Ships and Vessels at Plymouth, from a young Lieutenant, M.P.J.Rochfort, whom he had put in charge of the salvage, can be seen today in the Public Record Office at Kew. Rochfort was very keen. This is his first letter to the Admiral:

Hope Cutter, Salcomb Harbour.
16th May, 1784.

Sir,

I proceeded with his Majesty's Cutter Hope under my command agreeable to your orders to Prawl Point and on our arrival there we found the Crocodile with nothing standing except her Bowsprit; laying almost down on her Beam-Ends in an irrecoverable State.

Afterwards I proceeded to save as much of her Stores as possible; but owing to a very high sea rising, we were not able to work until the 13th instant and for the purpose of employing all my people I thought it advisable to bring the Hope in here, it being a convenient place to carry on a communication between the Wreck and us. I intend to send one of the Yard Lighters back with such of her Stores as we have saved as soon as these Spring tides are over which is the most favourable time for us to work on the Wreck. I will acquaint you with any further proceedings and I hope to be able to save her Guns, Anchors, Cables, and some Sails.

I am,
Sir,
Your very humble servant,
Lieut. M.P.J. Rochfort.
Hope Cutter.

Lieutenant Rochfort was full of enthusiasm for his task, but it wasn't as simple as he first thought. A week later his tune had changed. His second letter to the Admiral, was dated May 22 :

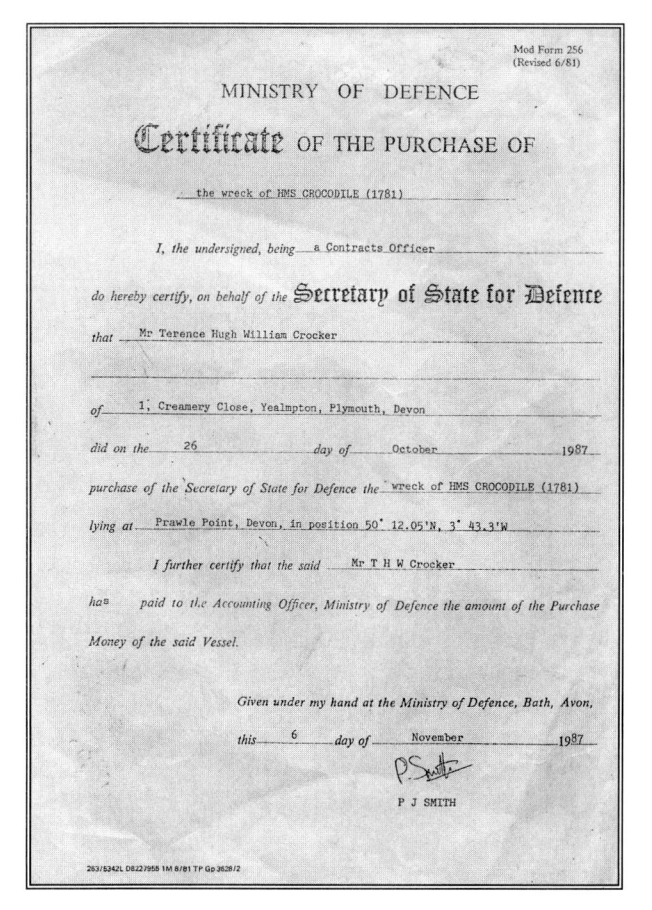

Sir,

I beg leave to acquaint you that it was not in my power to save as much of the Crocodile's Stores as I at first expected and have only saved what is mentioned in the enclosed. The Sails in the Sail Room were overset and entangled in the Water with each other. The Cables in the Orlop in the same situation and all on her larboard side, which she lays on, the men not having a place to stand to work, added further to the difficulty of saving them. I think it adviseable to send to Plymouth the largest of the Lighters (as she may be wanted) with such of the Crocodile's Stores as are saved. The small one I propose waiting here until the next Spring tides at which time I am in hopes of saving her Anchors and the remainder of her Guns, and as the Lighters might be lost in attempting to get them out, I thought it adviseable to hire Mr. Ball of this place to Assist with his Craft. As the Helena is now in Exmouth Harbour I propose leaving this place tomorrow and proceed to my station with the Hope until a day or two before the next Spring tides.

With that letter Lieutenant Rochfort enclosed a list of the stores he had saved so far headed: **A List of His Majesty's Stores saved from the Crocodile and sent in the Tortoise Lighter to Plymouth.**

Iron Ordnance 9 Pdrs..............Thirteen.
Iron Ordnance 6 Pdrs................One.
Iron Ordnance carriages..........Fourteen.
Bayonets...................................Fifty one.
Cutlasses..................................Fifty five.
Musquets..................................Sixty six.
Cartouch boxes........................Thirty two.
Spunges....................................Five.
Lade...One.
Worm...One.
Junk..Twenty one lengths.
Sails..Eight or ten.
Spar..One.
Top Gallt.Mast..........................One.
Coppers and Funnell
2 Chain pump wheels and a number of lengths and different sorts of Iron-work.

There the written record of Rochfort's salvage appears to end. But there is little doubt that he got up all except one of her cannon before the next gales smashed the *Crocodile* into pieces. Divers of today have found the badly rusted remains of only one cannon in a gully close to Prawle Island. It is still there on the left-hand side of the Island as you look down on *Crocodile*'s grave from the Point.

Foot Note: The minutes of the court-martial of Patrick Crawley in great stern cabin of *HMS Princess Royal* in Portsmouth Harbour on June 7,1784, can be seen in the Public Record Office at Kew. Despite the fact that they were taken down with a quill pen at great speed during the trial, the copper-plate writing is almost without a fault on any of the pages.

The wreck of the *Crocodile* now belongs to diver Terry Crocker of Yealmpton, who bought her scattered remains in 1987, from the Ministry of Defence for £50. His certificate of ownership is reproduced on page 103.

He has raised bronze keel pins marked with the Navy's broad arrow, musket balls, pan weights, barbed nails for wood, sounding leads, a rudder pintle, and discovered under the wreckage of the *Heye-P* (see Wreck No. 52) a whole "bed" of cannon balls.

54. DEMETRIOS
Prawle Point, 1992

PRAWLE comes from an old English word for a lookout, and that is exactly what Prawle Point provides today, with a big Coastguard Station, at the most southerly point in Devon. Whether the fact that the Point juts out so far into the Channel has anything to do with it or not, the fact is that there have been more recorded shipwrecks in the vicinity than on any comparable short stretch of coast in the country.

In fact local divers were quite upset when, on December 18,1992, yet another wreck was added to the wrecks of the Prawle and sprawled right across several interesting and much older wreck sites. The newcomer was the 9700-ton cargo ship *Demetrios*, formerly the Chinese-owned *Longlin*, which was being towed from Dunkirk by a Russian tug,*Nastoroh*, to a Turkish breaker's yard. That tow parted 16 miles off Start Point in a Force Ten gale. A second tug tried to get a line aboard, but failed.

The *Demetrios*, with no one aboard, was then blown by the great wind for five hours before crashing into Prawle Point, just by Gull Island. Massive seas broke her in half. She is now draped along the cliffs (see front and rear pictures).

The news of the wreck spread a great deal faster in these tv days than it could have done long ago, but the result was the same. In an incredible flashback to the bad old days, thousands came from miles around to see the wreck. They turned East Prawle into a giant traffic jam and the police had to close the road down to Prawle Point. But the wreck still drew the people down to her. Their feet marked out a great earth-mud road across the grass and you could see how it had been at many another wreck centuries ago. And to make the comparison complete, there was looting from the *Demetrios* as some among the thousands who went to see her climbed aboard from the rocks!

Foot Note:Prawle Point is well over 300ft high and has an arch at the tip at sea level. Prawle Island is the big rock almost attached to the Point and slightly to the west. North from the Island is Gull Rock, which lives up to its name being usually crowded with seagulls. Those with a good imagination will spot "The Horse", whose head can be made out of the rocks of the actual Point, though this is best pictured from a boat at sea to the west.

55. DE BOOT.
Gull Rock, 1738.

THE bowsprit of *De Boot* came out of the mist of the early morning of October 20,1738, and speared Gull Rock dead centre. The ash of the bowsprit shattered and the rest of the 130 wooden feet of the Dutch East Indiaman ploughed into the rocks of Prawle Point. The next wave powered by the south-westerly gale picked her up again and drove her even further on. Two crewmen lost their grip and were washed to their deaths on the rocks.

Almost as soon as she struck Captain Jacob van Duijnen knew that his ship was lost. The grinding and crackling beneath the deck on which he stood told him that. Now his job was to save what cargo he could. The tea in which thousands of pieces of Ming porcelain were cushioned would wash away. The Chinese porcelain would probably all smash. But there were 12 small wooden boxes packed tight in sealed lockers in his cabin which could, and must be, saved.

Captain van Duijnen had sailed *De Boot* out of Rotterdam bound for Batavia on April 2,1738. The ship and her 80 crew had been chartered by the Amsterdam, Horn and Enkuigen Chambers of the Dutch East India Company from the Rotterdam Chamber for the round trip to the East.

Her odd name simply meant "The Boat". At the time she was built in the early 1700s, the Dutch East India Company had a thing about calling their ships "The" this and "The" that. *De Liefde* (The Love) wrecked in 1711 in the Shetlands, *De Snoek* (The Pike), *De Schaap* (The Sheep), *De Aap* (The Monkey), *Den Berg* (The Mountain) and *De Witte Leeuw* (The White Lion) are other examples of "De" names for the Company's ships.

The 650-ton *De Boot* had delivered the Company stores safely to Batavia and had then been loaded with tea and porcelain and those 12 small wooden boxes. They were crammed full of uncut diamonds and rubies! Her cargo was worth 250,000 pounds sterling. Or so her captain told the Exeter correspondent of The Sherborne Mercury after the wreck.

Now as his ship started to break up underneath him and several of her 40 cannon careered loose across the gun deck, he knew that all he had left to save were those precious stones. Even if he did save them, the Gentlemen of the Company would still have lost much of their investment. But the safe delivery of the jewel stones, he knew, might just enable him to be allowed to serve in another of the East India Company's ships.

Rollers smashed down on her stern and then swept on over her deck. Despite this a chain of sailors managed to pass those boxes of stones along a line from the captain's stern cabin to the bow and then finally dropped them down to Roeloff Blok, the First Mate, who had taken charge of a little group of sailors who had already got ashore on to the rocks.

Local people, mostly the villagers of East Prawle, were now slithering down the steep slopes of Prawle Point to reach the wreck, though there was little they could do to save anything of the ship or anyone from it - even if that had been their intention.

The seas were even bigger now. As Captain Duijnen watched anxiously the transfer of the little boxes, he suddenly saw that Paulus Schults, the ship's book-keeper,

The Captain dropped the box of diamonds into the man's hands.

was scrabbling about on the bow and actually noting down each package on a slate as it went off the ship. Would he have taken such care if the packages had merely held salt pork? Having known Schults since they had first set sail for Batavia, the Captain decided that he would.

It was time to leave. The Captain picked up the last of the little boxes himself and was surprised how heavy it was. However, the weight helped him to keep his feet as he made his way to the bow. Looking down he saw one of the locals, who, braver than the rest, had pushed forward until the water was up to his neck and he was almost under the bow. As a wave foamed over his head and then crashed on the rocks behind him, the man held up his hands and the Captain dropped the box into them. As he waited to make sure he was the last to leave his ship, the Captain saw the man with the box struggle safely to shore. Though he didn't know it then it was the last he was to see of that particular box and that particular man!

That was not the only theft from the wreck. The Sherborne Mercury and Weekly Advertiser in its edition of November 21, 1738, describes the theft of the diamonds like this:

"Large Quantities of Tea and other valuable Goods (Part of the Cargo of the Dutch India Man lost off the Praul Head the 20th of last Month) have been taken up along Shore from Exmouth to Beare. Her Cargo by Report of the Captain was worth near 250,000l. Sterling. Part of which consisted in Diamonds; one of the Boxes in which they were contained, being by the Captain delivered to a Countryman, the Fellow had the Modesty to march off with the same, and has not been since heard of.

"A Man is committed for stealing Iron from the said Ship, who has given in a List of a great Number concerned in those vile Practices."

Foot Note: That man was obviously trying to save himself from the noose by informing on his partners. The "Iron" of the ship refers to her 40 cannon, of which no trace can be found by divers today - unless the much corroded six-footer in a nearby gully is hers and not from *HMS Crocodile*.

However, there is no doubt that Gull Rock marks the site of the wreck. Robert Stenuit, the famous Belgian underwater archaeologist, who raised the treasures of the *Girona*, a ship of the Spanish Armada, wrecked in Ireland in 1588, proved that. He dug trenches underwater across the seabed around Gull Rock for much of one summer and was disappointed not to find a single intact piece of porcelain from *De Boot*'s cargo. But he did create a Ming seabed gleaming and glistening with tiny shards of the broken blue and white porcelain which he unearthed.

If you scramble down to Gull Rock today, you can often find some of those shards for yourself amid the rock pools, stones and sand. Take care. Sudden waves do rush in. Keep your eyes open on your way for a pile of small white stones. It is highly likely that the man who stole the uncut diamonds was most disappointed when he opened the box to find a lot of old stones in it. He probably threw them away!

56. RIVERSDALE
Off Prawle, 1917.

CORNELIUS Simms, the gunner of the *Riversdale*, kissed goodbye to a quiet Christmas when he pumped four shells at the periscope he thought he saw a little way off to port. It was a good try. The 12-pounder shells exploded close enough to the periscope of *UB-31* to make Oberleutnant Bieber curse and dive.

But the quick reaction of Simms brought a similar reaction from Bieber as all aboard the *Riversdale* found out a few minutes later into that crisp day of December 18, 1917, when a torpedo slammed into the ship's port side near the bow. Almost immediately after the explosion, the sea started to fill No.1 hold.

The 2805-ton British steamer was just a mile south of Prawle Point when she was torpedoed. A 317ft-long steel single-screw ship, she had been on her way from the Tyne for Savona, Italy with a cargo of 4000 tons of coal for the Italian State Railways.

Though water was pouring into her, Captain John Thorn Simpson thought he had a good chance of beaching her and headed for Elender Cove, just to the east of Gammon Head at full speed. After a few minutes of that he felt she was holding up well and changed his mind and turned to head for Plymouth. She didn't like that and started to heel over and fill more rapidly. Captain Simpson switched back to his original plan and made for the shore.

He was lucky that Bieber in *UB-31* had not stayed around, possibly because of Cornelius and his 12-pounder, but headed away submerged to the north-east in search of other targets. He may also, of course, have thought the *Riversdale* was a total loss - as she took the ground in Elender Cove, one of the stoves in the forecastle tipped over and smoke and flames poured out of the portholes.

It was, however, a minor fire and soon put out. Biggest problem was to stop the ship swinging broadside on. Anchors were placed fore and aft, but wouldn't hold her. When the tug *Woonda* arrived and put a large cable on her, it parted and the *Riversdale* swung on to the rocks. However, her crew of 28 and two RNR gunners, Cornelius Simms and Arthur Barber, were all saved.

She had been built by J. Blumer and Co, of Sunderland in 1906 and was a strong ship. The place Captain Simpson had put his ship was well chosen even though she had hit the rocks. It enabled salvage crews to work on her.

Salvage experts were convinced she could be saved. So a good deal of her coal was thrown overboard. She was pumped out. Then her bulkheads were shored up, and air compressors were installed on her decks to counter the pressure of the sea on the patched-up torpedo hole. Tugs started to pull her off, stern first.

She came clear without much trouble at 6.15 a.m. on December 28. But before she had been towed 1,000 yards, she ran into a confused swell and seas began to break over her. The torpedo patch must have given way because 20 minutes later she started to sink by the bow and disappeared in a mass of bubbles. Today she is in deep water - over 100 feet - just off the Point She sits upright on the seabed and that is how she was found by the Torbay divers of the British Sub-Aqua Club.

Foot Note: The divers identified her by means of the letters 'HGMR' amateurishly centre-punched on to one of the spokes of a small bronze wheel they had raised. These turned out to be the *Riversdale*'s wartime signal letters. Having identified her the Torbay divers then approached the Ministry of Transport in 1964 to see if they could buy her. War loss compensation to the owners had already been paid so the Ministry asked for an offer. As a joke Torbay said "a fiver". To their amazement it was accepted!

SECTION FIVE –
Landing Cove to Start Point

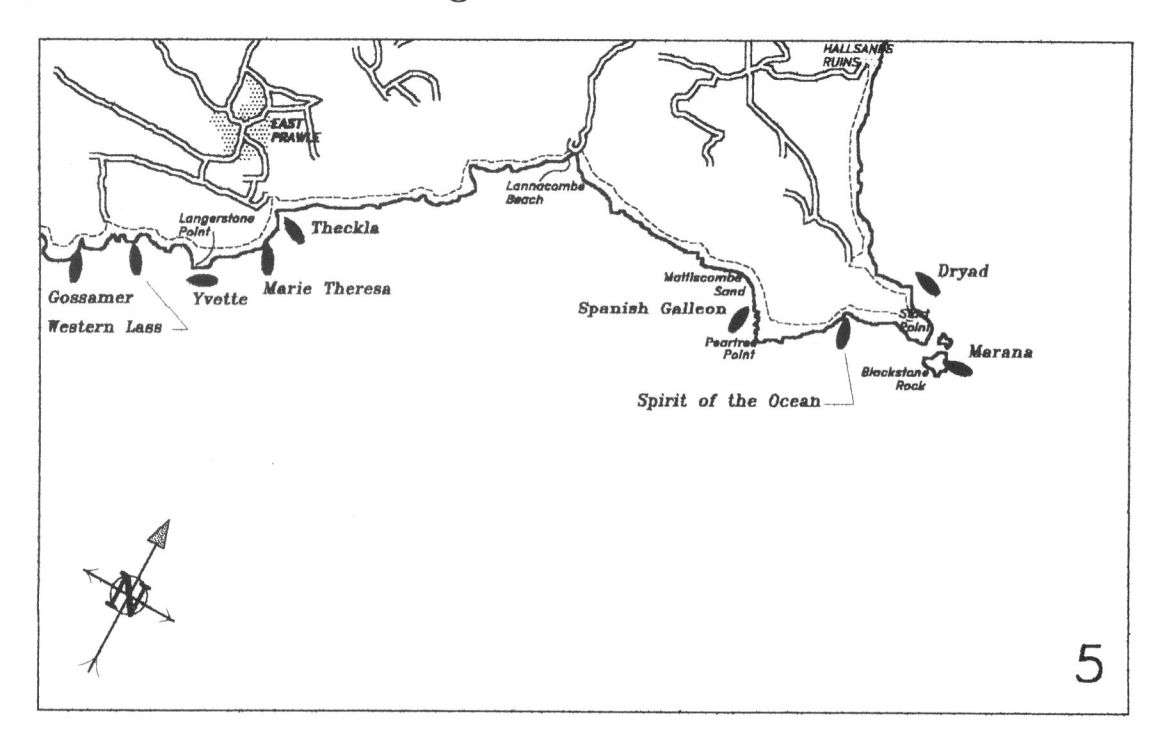

57. GOSSAMER.
Landing Cove, 1868.

CAPTAIN John Thomson and Barbara, his bride of only 14 days, were just two of the 13 who were killed in the wreck of this big tea clipper in a Force Nine gale from the south-south-west on Thursday, December 10, 1868. The captain and his young wife died in each other's arms.

The mighty wind drove the *Gossamer* on to the rocks just one hundred yards short of Landing Cove to the east of Prawle Point. Some of her remains are still in the rock pools left behind when the tide goes out.

A 734-ton fully-rigged China clipper, she was 181 feet long with a beam of 30ft. Apart from her speed - she had been the second ship home from China in the annual tea-race from Shanghai to London only two months before she was wrecked - she was famous too because she was one of the few composite ships built in Britain - that means she had an iron frame and wood planked sides.

Ships made of wood and iron had been built as early as 1814, but they all suffered from corrosion between the iron and the brass bolts which held the ship together It wasn't until 1861 that Lloyds finally agreed that ships built in this way could qualify for the Lloyds 15-year A1 certificate. In the lead of this kind of composite building were Alexander

Stephen and Sons of Kelvinborough, Glasgow. They built the *Gossamer* in 1864.

At the time of the wreck, the *Gossamer* was outward-bound for Adelaide, Australia and carried the captain, his wife, 24 crew, four passengers and a general cargo. Also on board when she was towed out of London docks and down the Thames Estuary by the tug *Middlesex* on Wednesday, December 2 was their Channel pilot, Andrew Grant of London. The weather was bad right from the start, so much so that they had to shelter in The Downs for a week until the next Wednesday morning. Then a moderate north wind helped them down Channel despite heavy seas. The wind then swung into a strong south-westerly gale. Despite this, by Thursday morning, December 10, they were nine miles off Start Point. Captain John Thomson, who had been on deck most of Tuesday night, all day Wednesday and most of that night coping with stormy seas, went below to rest.

While he slept, *Gossamer* continued to tack down Channel. Just before he went below Captain Thomson had asked his Chief Officer, Peter Merrifield, if he thought the ship would get round Start and Prawle Point on their present tack.

"Not unless there is more canvas on her," said Mr. Merrifield.

"I think she will," said the Captain.

The Chief Officer was unhappy about this decision, but with the Captain below, the Pilot was in charge. After a while, Merrifield noted with concern that the ship was making a great deal of leeway towards the shore. Not only that, he could see that the current which runs between Start and Prawle and sweeps in round the shore, was also pulling the ship in towards the cliffs of Prawle. He pointed this out to the Pilot, who replied that the Captain had said she would go round. He didn't think she would, but he was going to try it.

Merrifield once again urged that they should put up more sail, pointing out that she was barely making three knots and that the leeway was increasing. When the Pilot made no reply, Peter Merrifield felt he had to call the Captain, who was in his cabin with his wife. When he got no reply he went to the poop and told the Pilot that they had barely room left to wear the ship around on the other tack.

The Pilot now seemed to see the danger and ordered the Chief to set the main topsails and the inner jib. Merrifield called all hands and got them aloft setting sail. He then called the Captain again. This time John Thomson replied he would be up directly.

By the time he appeared on deck it was too late. They tried to tack, but the ship hadn't got enough way on her to come round.. "My God, why didn't they call me before?" said the Captain. Prawle Point loomed over them, less than half-a-mile away.

The Pilot ordered an anchor to be dropped. It held and 90 fathoms (540 feet) of anchor cable raced out. The Captain ordered a second one down, but the Pilot said: "Don't or you'll lose both anchors at once!" But the second anchor had to go down when they came to the end of the cable of the first. Even though it held, the *Gossamer* struck almost immediately after it was dropped.

It was now 2.15 p.m. Huge seas began to break over the ship and though all boats were ordered to be launched, there was no way it could be done. The cable of the second anchor parted five minutes later. The clipper was free again. She drifted in towards the land for another 15 minutes.

On shore, the coastguards of Prawle had seen the whole tragedy unfold below them. James Pengelly, the Coastguard Chief Officer of Prawle, had seen her round the Start at about one p.m. She was then some three to five miles off shore. As she came nearer to the coastguard station she was making so much leeway that she was barely half a mile out. When she was still a mile away, he called out his rocket team. He knew what was going to happen.

She missed Landing Cove, the only stretch of sand and shingle which might have cushioned her, by just one hundred yards and struck fore and aft on the low rocks of the shore. The surf boiled around her and over her and she started breaking up almost at once. The first of the big waves to sweep over her took away the boats and anything loose on the deck. She was only 300 feet from the shore and a number of the crew jumped overboard as soon as the first breakers fell back and started to swim and scramble over the rocks. The next wave beat them under and most were drowned almost immediately.

The first shot of the rocket apparatus went over her, but the men left on deck didn't seem to have the strength to haul the hawser aboard. At 2.45 p.m. Merrifield and some other members of the crew got ashore by using the thin handline of the rocket and being dragged to safety by the coastguards.

Nineteen of those aboard were saved. But not the Captain and his wife, Barbara. Those on shore watched in horror as they were left clinging to the rails near the stern. One of the crew, a black man, who was known to everyone on board as a magnificent swimmer, clawed his way to them and offered to take the captain's wife ashore on his back. But the Captain refused to trust her to anyone else. The sailor swam ashore with ease. As he landed a tremendous sea crashed over the deck and tore his wife from the Captain's encircling arms. The Captain flung himself into the foam after her and managed to reach her before both disappeared amid the white water. They were still clasped together when their bodies were washed ashore two hours later.

After such a tragedy there was much talk of how such a fine ship could have been wrecked in such a stupid manner. Who was to blame? Most acrimony was directed at Andrew Grant, the ship's pilot.

Not all the bodies were found, but those which were washed ashore were kept in the belfry of Chivelstone's St. Sylvester Church so that the jury could see them before hearing the witnesses at the inquest held in the Seven Stars Inn at Chivelstone.

After hearing most of the evidence Mr. Bone of Devonport, the Coroner, asked Andrew Grant, the Pilot on the *Gossamer* if he wished to give evidence, cautioning him that he need not do so. Grant, who had taken the precaution, of having Mr. John Square of Kingsbridge, his solicitor, present, said that if Captain Thomson was alive, he would have absolved him from blame as he was only acting as the Captain's assistant at the time as he was beyond the limits of his pilotage.

At the end of the inquest, the Coroner summed up, pointing out that if the pilot, through gross negligence or gross ignorance had occasioned the loss of the ship, he would be guilty of manslaughter. His solicitor, Mr. Square, had urged that he was not responsible when outside his limits, but he had continued to give orders, therefore he, the coroner, considered he was still responsible as pilot.

It took the jury only a few minutes to bring in a verdict of manslaughter against the pilot, who was committed to Devon Assizes in Exeter, but was allowed bail with two sureties of £100 each and his own of £150, a total of £350 in all.

Andrew Grant appeared for trial in Exeter in the week of March 7, 1869, and the judge is reported as telling the grand jury that it was clear that Grant was out of his district. If the pilot had been in charge of the ship within his own district, he, the judge, thought they would expect a higher degree of skill than they would from a man who was in charge simply at the request of the Captain, out of his district and not having so much knowledge as he would of his own district. The Captain had remained below with his wife and although there had been a gale blowing and the Mate had been to him several times, he did not go on deck until very late indeed. The pilot had been perfectly sober and was doing his best. It was not at all clear that he was in charge as the Mate gave some orders and the Captain when he came on deck interfered and gave directions about the anchors.

Today the Judge's words read like a clear direction to the jury that there was no case to answer. But the Devon Assizes jury still persisted that they wanted to hear the case against the pilot. However, it is reported that after hearing all the evidence, the jury finally dismissed the case against Andrew Grant.

The speed with which the ship broke up - less than three hours - was immediately seized upon as evidence of a weakness of composite building. The wiseacres said that her bottom had come away as soon as she struck leaving her deck and topsides to float ashore, something that they were sure would never have happened with a timber-framed ship. However, the loss of the *Gossamer* was never used as evidence further afield of any weakness in the composite ships and many other clippers were built by this method, which finally died out in the 1880s.

Foot Note: A solitary black tombstone on the grass to the left of the main door of Chivelstone Church marks the grave of the Captain and his love. It bears the words:

ERECTED

IN

MEMORY OF

CAPT_N. JOHN THOMSON

A NATIVE OF ROTHESAY, ISLE OF BUTE

AND OF HIS WIFE

BARBARA KERR

WHO WERE UNFORTUNATELY DROWNED

IN THE MELANCHOLY SHIPWRECK OF

THE "GOSSAMER", NEAR PRAWLE POINT

10TH DECEMBER 1868.

———

IN THE MIDST OF LIFE, WE ARE IN DEATH

Several of the others lost in the wreck are also buried at Chivelstone, whose church dates back to the 13th century and is worth a visit to see not only the tombstone, but also the pulpit, which is carved out of a solid oak tree trunk, and there is an ancient iron ring for claiming sanctuary set in the main door.

The Seven Stars Inn is no more. The inn is now a private house, right next door to the graveyard.

As you look down from Prawle Point on to the area around Landing Cove, imagine the scene just after the wreck. Because of her quick break-up, the ship's timbers and crates of her £50,000 cargo were soon spread all along the rocks. And hundreds of looters arrived almost as quickly. The Kingsbridge Gazette of December 24 describes it well: **"The plundering which has taken place at this wreck is certainly worthy of the days of old Cornwall and the representatives of the underwriters are quite justified in making examples of the more flagrant cases. It is high time that persons should be taught that wrecked goods are not public property. Many of the residents of the adjoining villages are reported as already having large stores of stolen property.**

"The wreck of this noble vessel now lies scattered about in some eight or ten pieces on the magnificent belt of rocks that rings the Prawle coast, on the eastern side of the Point. The margin of the cove is almost covered with the debris of the wreck, put into large heaps and broken into such small fragments as to be valuable only as firewood, whilst in the fields above are lots of ropes, sacks, casks, and such torn and tangled portions of calico, linens, sailcloth and wearing apparel as were not worth shipping off to a better market.

"An extemporised wooden house shelters the more valuable portions of the cargo and stores a collection of books, cloth, furniture, shoes, nails, blankets, calicos, cheese, bonnets, boots and shoes, and general merchandise.

"The general appearance of the spot is most striking. The carriage of the more valuable portions of the cargo up the steep slopes of the precipitous cliffs has created highways and roads, but are still so steep as to be only surmountable by the wiry little horses that belong to the farmers in the neighbourhoods, who have reaped a second harvest.

"Viewed from the top of the cliff, the scene resembles a large military encampment, the huge piles of multicoloured merchandise bear the likeness of so many tents spread over the many acres of open ground, while open fires were lit here and there for cooking purposes, throwing their bright and weird lights over the surrounding objects".

During the following few days, the whole of that material was auctioned on the edge of the sea. That sale "collected a congregation of not less than a thousand people, comprising representatives of all classes of society". A party of brokers from Plymouth were the main buyers of the bits of the ship and were after the bronze bolts, which had held the iron frame to the teak planking.

On the last day of the auction when the auctioneer tried to sell the whole of the rest of the torn and wet drapery and materials as one lot, the crowd of over 500 became angry and said they couldn't afford it. One man threatened the auctioneer saying he would find himself "over cleave"(chopped up). Hastily the auctioneer offered the material, carpets and rugs, in small lots. To his surprise they all went for very high prices.

Said the Kingsbridge Gazette at the weekend: **"The village of Prawle resembles a place under sack by the enemy. The two little publics are crowded to such an extent that reasonable provision from either of them is an utter impossibility, and the access to the village is bad from the wretched condition of the roads. It will take some days, possibly weeks, before the whole of the property is entirely removed from the beaches, but judging from the avidity with which the country people are buying up the heaps of rags at the high prices which competition enlisted, the whole of the wreckage will probably be converted into circulating medium during the week".**

Some locals, however, had not paid for the materials which they carried away. They were caught. Local magistrates fined many of them - a man £1 7s 6d for taking 18 pairs of boots; a woman 14s 6d for looting a shirt, two jackets, a vest and a pair of men's drawers. But many got away with it. "Gossamer" dresses were the height of fashion among local ladies for many years!

Today, some small pieces from the *Gossamer* can be found in rock pools and gullies on the shore. Take care: the seabed falls steeply quite close in. Local diver Stephen George has recovered many items - brass bolts stamped "A.S&S", blocks, inkwells (still full), cruet sets, compass supports shaped like dolphins, door knobs, dividers, and dinner plates.

58. WESTERN LASS.
Willow Cove, 1916

THIS wreck was indirectly the cause of the Salcombe Lifeboat disaster of October 27, 1916 when 13 lifeboatmen died (see Wreck No. 39).

It was not yet dawn when Mr Leonard Albert Charles May, chief officer of the coastguard stationed at Prawle Point was woken by one of his men. He was told that the men on watch had seen a blue light of distress appear in the dark approximately where the Meg Rock lies off Langerstone Point. It was 5.12 a.m. Mr.May immediately called out the crew of his rocket apparatus and sent a telephone message to Salcombe - "C.O. Prawle to S.L.Salcombe. Signal of distress on Meg Rock Langerstone Point."

The ship which had set off the blue light distress signal was the *Western Lass*, which had been heading for her home port of Plymouth in ballast when she was caught by the south-westerly gale and driven inshore. The schooner, however, was not on the Meg Rocks. In fact she missed them by inches and grounded in a little sandy beach the only piece of sand for miles around.

The coastguards said later that had she struck Meg Rock, nothing could have saved her and the only chance the crew would have had would have been to be picked up by the lifeboat. In fact, the rocket apparatus team found her in Willow Cove, got a line across her with the first shot, and by 6.45. had rescued all the crew. The rocket team got back to the station at 7.40 only to see the lifeboat sail at great speed past the point. They had no means of contacting her in that huge gale, though they saw her turn back once she had seen the wreck and the rocket lines hanging from her.

Foot Note: No one quite knows why the Meg Rock should be so named. It could be that fishermen caught the flatfish they still call "meg" here; the fish is properly called "megrim" and is rarely found in such shallow water.

The Yvette - a helicopter saved her captain. Picture: South Hams Newspapers.

59. YVETTE.
Langerstone Point, 1978.

MIKE Thomas looked down from the helicopter which had just plucked him to safety off his wrecked ship and knew that she was finished.

Only a few hours earlier, on March 12, 1978, the £35,000 Brixham trawler *Yvette* had been working her way along the coast heading for the fishing grounds off the Eddystone Lighthouse. At the helm then, with his eyes fixed on the radar had been one of the four aboard, crewman Chris Lidstone. Shortly after 5 a.m. he suddenly realised that the radar was not working properly. Seconds later she struck one of the underwater rocks of Langerstone Point.

The crash woke the rest of the crew, Noel Cattel, Ron Pallar, and owner-skipper Mike Thomas, and brought them racing on deck. Mike Thomas immediately sent off a May-Day call. The wind and a huge swell it had brought with it was pushing them further in to more rocks.

Prawle Point Coastguards received the call and sent their rocket team and apparatus to the cliffs above the wreck. Station Officer Jack Appleton studied the weather anxiously - the wind seemed to be increasing by the minute. But he waited to give the Salcombe lifeboat a chance to pull the trawler clear. This attempt failed. Then a Dutch salvage tug with special heavy-lift towing gear tried. But the 65ft, 40-ton trawler wouldn't budge. There was no more time and as the trawler started to list over to 80 degrees, Jack Appleton ordered the crew off. The first shot from the rocket apparatus fell right over her and the three crewmen were winched ashore in the breeches buoy. But before Mike Thomas could use the same escape route, the wind and seas became too strong. A radio call for a helicopter brought a reply from a Royal Navy frigate, *HMS Charybdis*, which by chance was not far away at sea. She flew off her Wasp helicopter and Mike Thomas was winched up off his ship, the first ship he had ever owned and which had been his for only 18 months. Another later storm broke the *Yvette* up completely

Foot Note: Remains of the *Yvette* can still be seen at low tide to the east of Landing Cove amid the widespread rocks of Langerstone Point.

It is interesting to note that the three men rescued from the *Yvette* were taken for shelter to the Pig's Nose Inn at East Prawle, as so many other shipwrecked sailors had been during earlier years when it was known as the Union Inn.

60. MARIE THERESA.
Brimpool Rocks, 1872

THIS ship is notable for the strange story of what happened after the wreck, ending with one of her crew cut down with swords by the Prawle coastguards after he went beserk. The wreck itself was a fairly calm affair, as wrecks go, or so it seemed at the time...

The Italian brig *Marie Theresa* was loaded with 850 tons of coal at Newcastle and left South Shields, heading for her home port of Genoa, on November 26, 1872. On December 4, she was 15 miles west of Start Point when a schooner rammed her port side. After the collision, the schooner, which was never named, sailed on, leaving the *Marie Teresa* leaking badly and only keeping afloat by manning the pumps all night. The next morning she was seen by the Prawle Point coastguard close in with a few sails set on a flat calm sea. A Salcombe pilot boat was called out, but Captain Nicolo Bozza of the Italian ship would not allow the pilot on board. Half an hour later the *Marie Theresa* was impaled on the Brimpool Rocks, near Dutch End, and was abandoned by her crew, who rowed for the shore and landed safely in Horseley Cove.

Captain Bozza said that he had put his ship on the rocks to save her from sinking. It wasn't a very good decision as that afternoon the wind rose, the sea came up, and by nightfall the brig was in pieces.

Later the Captain told what happened next: He and his crew had been sheltered in a house on the top of the cliff. Eleven of them went to the Union Inn in East Prawle for dinner and then went down to the scene of the wreck to see what could be saved. The crew started quarrelling on the seashore. As usual the crewman creating the quarrel was a Salvatore Ilavi, a 38-year-old able seaman, who had been with the ship for five and a half months and had caused nothing but trouble since he signed on. All the crew were afraid of him. Captain Bozza sighed as he heard Ilavi use his favourite proverb - "Ninety nine are mine and I am the hundredth" - it always meant that Salvatore was looking for trouble. He sent part of the crew, including the troublemaker, back to the house and stayed on the beach himself.

However, when Captain Bozza got back much later, everyone seemed to be in bed and asleep. He stayed up writing his report of the ship's loss and finally went to bed himself at 2 a.m. He hadn't been in bed long when the trouble started. And judging by the screams and yells it was big trouble. He told the landlord of the house to get the police, but there were none in the village and the man fetched a coastguard instead.

Ilavi had now got a knife, which one of the other seamen had been using to cut tobacco, and calling out "Dio mio, Dio mio, Dio mio", started trying to stab his shipmates. The arrival of the coastguard put a stop to that and Ilavi fled from the house. However, he went to the coastguard station and stabbed the duty coastguard five times, his wife three times and when another coastguard appeared stabbed him too.

Finally he was cornered by John Segrue, the Chief Boatman, and Henry Willcocks, the Commissioned Boatman. Segrue had a cutlass and Willcocks his tuck-stick, another name for a sword-stick. The demented sailor flung himself at them several times slashing out with the knife. One blow hit Segrue in the chest but deflected off a coat button. Segrue cut him down with a blow to his forehead and they wrenched the knife from him. But at the inquest it was revealed that the cutlass blow had not killed him. The post mortem showed that it was a thrust from Willcocks' tuck-stick blade in the back that had proved fatal.

The inquest jury found that "though the two coastguard men, Willcocks and Segrue, exceeded their duty, yet morally they considered they had done their duty and the deceased died from a wound given by Willcocks accidentally while attempting to disarm the man".

All those who had been stabbed later recovered.

Foot Note: The house in which the Italians stayed in the village and where the trouble started belonged to John Ambrose Patey, but today no one seems quite sure which one it is. The Union Inn is now The Pig's Nose, after a name change in 1949. The other inn in East Prawle is The Providence which dates back to 1807.

61. THECKLA.
Horseley Cove, 1891

ON May 8, 1891, a series of rogue waves hit the Swedish barque *Theckla*, captain John Peterson, as she was heading for Plymouth from Gottenburg with a cargo of deal and other wood boards. The huge waves were part of a strangely confused sea off Start Point driven up by a stiff breeze from the south-west.

One of the biggest waves struck her stern, broke her steering chains and almost tore away her rudder. The ship became uncontrollable and shortly after that her top sails were carried away. The seas now began to break on board washing the deck cargo overboard. The captain tried hard to repair the steering gear and finally managed to rig up a system of ropes. However, it took almost the entire crew of ten to steer the ship. During this the seas hit the ship with enormous force and she sprang a leak.

Even so she managed to weather the Start, but the lighthouse keeper spotted that she was in trouble and thought she was going to drive on shore. Somehow the crew managed to head her away until she came level with Prawle Point, where John Peterson gave up hope of keeping out at sea and ran in towards the coast looking for a safe place to beach. He saw nothing but rocks to the westward of Prawle and turned back.

The coastguards at Prawle saw what he was doing and signalled him to make for Horseley Cove, a little to the eastward of Sharpers Head. The 378-ton barque looked for a long time as though she would not make it and would end up on the Gorah Rocks even further to the east. Finally, however, she beached reasonably gently in Horseley Cove when the tide had been rising for an hour. The coastguards got the rocket apparatus ready, but the first two rockets missed the ship completely. The third was a perfect shot. The *Theckla*'s crew didn't know how to work the rocket lines, got in a terrible muddle, and made fast the gear to the ship so that the ropes couldn't move. They then launched their boat and landed safely.

The ship was 34 years old and was not insured. Captain Peterson said that there was about eight foot of water in her when they beached her. Even so he telegraphed to Plymouth for tugs. . The *Triumph* arrived late that evening and still later the *Vixen* put into Salcombe ready to start work early the next morning. They didn't get much chance. As the tide came up it lifted her further and further on to the rocks and she soon became a total wreck.

62. SPANISH GALLEON.
Peartree Point, 1700s

GREAT Mattiscombe Sand, a beach just round Peartree Point on the path towards Prawle, is known today by local families as "More Rope Bay". This strange name does gives strength to the tale of a foreign ship being wrecked here centuries ago. For there is a written story that the Rector of East Portlemouth Church was up in his pulpit and well into his sermon when his verger whispered into his ear that there was a ship ashore. Whereupon the Rector tore off his gown and shouted to his congregation: "Ship ashore near Peartree Point! Now steady, lads, just one more prayer. Let me get down and all start fair!"

The story adds that the ship was a Spanish galleon and the Rector and his congregation were much too concerned with looting the wreck than saving the crew who were struggling in the water or clinging to wreckage. "More rope, more rope" shouted the drowning men, for what rope was thrown to them was much too short to reach. It is terrible to think that this may have been deliberate, but one of the laws formulated for dealing with wrecks and the recoveries from them at that time clearly stated: "If any man or living thing escape to shore alive, it is no wreck". And so no one except a survivor could benefit from it. If the looters made sure that no man, woman, dog or cat reached the beach alive, then at the very least they could make a claim for salvage.

Nothing more is known about the "Spanish galleon". Some people have embellished the story by saying that those round mounds nearby are the graves of the crew, but they are in fact outcrops of flint, which show traces of having been worked by early man for tools.

Of course, the ship might have been French - for on the western side of Peartree Point is Frenchman's Rock!

63. SPIRIT OF THE OCEAN
Foxhole Cove, 1866

THE bravery of Samuel Popplestone of Start Farm at the wreck of the *Spirit of the Ocean* on March 23, 1866, led Queen Victoria to institute a new medal for gallantry for saving life at sea. She named the new medal after her husband - and so the Albert Medal came into being. Quite properly the first recipient of that medal was farmer Samuel Popplestone.

The *Spirit of the Ocean* was built in 1863, a barque of 578 tons. The 159-foot-long ship was quickly known as a fast sailer and this probably accounts for the fact that there were 24 passengers aboard with the crew of 18 when she left London for Halifax, Nova Scotia, with a general cargo, which included a large quantity of tea.

However, a letter handed to the Margate pilot boat by one of the passengers for delivery to a relative ashore, gives an unhappy picture of life aboard. He wrote: **"We have a motley crew of sailors and only a few of them able seamen. Most are landsmen, four are seasick. It is hard work for the mates. The passengers have had to lend a hand to weigh anchor and hoist sails...."**

It must have been worse when she headed further down Channel and ran straight into some appalling weather with gale-force winds from the north-east. By the time she was off the Devon coast she had lost or damaged most of her sails. Captain Roulle Cary tried to put into Dartmouth for shelter, but the wind drove him past the entrance and for a while he was embayed in Start Bay.

Once they had fought clear and rounded Start Point

with the ship under storm sails, Captain Cary put her on the port tack to try and get back to Dartmouth. He was only 400 yards west of Start Point when the gale increased and the trysail was torn to ribbons. Now they were at the mercy of the wind and there was no chance of clearing Start Point again, so Captain Cary put her head towards the small bay of Foxhole Cove, hoping to run in close under the cliff.

Mr. Samuel Popplestone, of Start Farm which is on the high ground above the Point, has seen the ship in trouble and immediately sent one of his men on horseback to warn the coastguards and, seizing a coil of rope, made for Foxhole Cove himself.

By the time he reached the cliff top, the *Spirit of the Ocean* had smashed on to a small reef of rocks just out from the shore. Within five minutes of striking she parted amidships and the bow turned bottom up and together with the stern portion floated right in to the cliff. As she struck half the passengers were swept overboard and the rest took shelter in a poop cabin where Creighton Jenkins, the Mate, joined them.

The top of the cabin very soon gave way. and as the vessel lay on her beam ends the cabin formed a deep well into which the sea broke and drowned all there, except for the Mate, and a Dr. Cooke who both held on for a long time to a berth and so were suspended above the water. The part to which Dr. Cooke was holding broke away and he fell and was engulfed.

Samuel Popplestone could see from the clifftop that there were still some people on part of the decking, though most of the wreck, which had been built of pine, was broken to pieces in the surf. Making his rope fast to an outcrop of rock, he lowered himself down to the narrow beach at the foot of the cliffs of the cove. He had a desperate struggle almost at once to keep his feet as huge timbers were being flung up across the strip of shingle. Two seaman made their way across this floating debris guided by Mr. Popplestone. Then he saw that there was a rocky ledge close to the stern portion of the wreckage, on which two men could be seen. One was the Mate, still clinging to the remains of the poop. Mr. Popplestone fought his way through the waves and across the slippery weeded rocks to the ledge. Once there he tried time and time again to get a rope across to the Mate. Once he was washed off the slippery weeded rocks, but managed to use the next wave to get himself back in place! Finally the Mate gripped the rope and Popplestone dragged him to shore.

The other man seemed in better shape than the Mate and once he had caught the line thrown to him was able to make more effort to help himself to safety. Mr. Popplestone guided the men to the rope hanging down the cliff face. But none of them had strength left to climb it. It wasn't until several hours later that a search party found the rope tied to the rock at the cliff top and hauled the men to safety. These were the only four survivors of the 42 aboard.

The *Spirit of the Ocean* was owned by Crawshaw of London, who valued her cargo at £50,000. There are reports of plundering after the wreck. One of the seamen who got ashore identified a chest as his and having claimed it left it for a short while on the cliff top. When he got back it had been broken open and the contents stolen. Soon there were many similar stories of looting at the wreck site and the coastguards were fully occupied trying to stop it.

The force of the storm was obvious. When the weather calmed down, it was seen that most of the wood of the barque had been broken into firewood and her iron knees snapped in half at their thickest part. Despite that it is surprising to learn that two days after the week "a cat and two canary birds" were taken out of the stern section still alive.

Divers were at work on the wreck during the first week of April and raised a large part of her cargo.

The survivors told everyone of the gallantry of Mr. Popplestone. And the Kingsbridge Gazette of April 7 commented: **We cannot omit a special reference to the conduct of Mr. Popplestone thoughout this fearful time. Those who are acquainted with him are aware that his actions are governed by Christian principle and therefore he will say and feel that he has only done as he would wish to be done by. But it is right. The publishers know that to** his untiring exertions at the risk of his own life the four men who were rescued are indebted for their safety, refreshment and shelter during the night. Those only who have seen the spot can realise the peril in which Mr.Popplestone stood when engaged in his noble work. Surely he deserves the Gold Medal if ever man did.

Foot Note: The reef on which the *Spirit of the Ocean* first struck can be seen at low tide to the right of centre of Foxhole Cove and almost exactly 100 yards offshore.

Mr. F.Kellock, the Deputy Coroner, held an inquest on the bodies at Stokenham. The jury's verdict:"Accidentally drowned". At Stokenham where the bodies lie in the churchyard, you can see a large stained glass memorial window in the south transcept of the Church to those lost in the wreck. It is appropriately inscribed: "The Lord is mightier than the mighty waves of the sea", but, surprisingly, you have to look hard - at the angels' sashes - to see the words "Spirit of the Ocean".

64. MARANA
Blackstone Rock, 1891.

THE Great Blizzard of 1891 struck the West Country on March 9. It was totally unexpected. February had been mild and dry with many days that could only be described as warm. The first week of March was like that. The crocuses were well out and butterflies fluttered around the primroses. On Sunday, March 8, the wind from the North-East felt cold. On the Monday morning the wind stopped and the temperature dropped to freezing. At 11 a.m. the wind came back, but this time it was from the South-East. Soon it had reached hurricane force. And with it came the snow.

To say that Britain was caught napping was an understatement. The blizzard trapped people in the open and they froze to death. Telephone lines came down as the poles snapped like matchsticks. Lanes filled with snow to the hedgetops. Sheep on cliff farms were blown into the sea. One coastguard at Start said that you couldn't see the sea for the foam.

The biggest casualty in the South Hams of the Blizzard of '91 was the single-funnel steamer *Marana*. Built of iron by Aitken and Mansel in Glasgow in 1880, she was also schooner-rigged and was designed to use her sails to save coal by steadying her and adding to her speed when the winds were favourable. Most steamers of the time had masts and sails for this reason.

The *Marana* of 1692 tons was 285 feet long with a beam of 36ft. Her owners, George Bell and Company of Liverpool, used her to carry cargoes all over the world. She left London's Victoria Docks on March 1,1891, bound for Colombo, Ceylon (Sri Lanka today) with a crew of 28 and a general cargo, mostly consisting of 2,000 wooden railway sleepers and telegraph poles. Captain Higginson was under orders to call at Swansea for coal before heading south

However, he was delayed in the Downs and did not start to cross Lyme Bay until the morning of the 9th March. She was off St.Catherine's Point when the blizzard struck her. At 3 p.m. Chief Officer Edward Browning ordered all her sails down and stowed, though because of the wind force her speed actually increased. It was bitterly cold and the snow was coming at them level across the sea like swarms of white midges. It was almost impossible to see anything.

A coastguard at Hallsands described conditions like this:"We did our utmost to keep our eyes open and strained them in the face of the storm, but the effort was so painful that we had to desist. The force of the storm was so great that our eyes seemed as if they were being pricked with needles and they were still bloodshot the next morning".

But despite this, the Hallsands coastguard did spot the *Marana*. She appeared for a few fleeting moments in a partial lull in the snow. The coastguard thought she was behaving strangely. She was dangerously close to the Skerries Bank, a shoal of sand and shingle starting about 1200 yards to the north-east of Start Point. The Skerries are in places only six feet deep. In the tremendous seas which boiled over them, the *Marana* was likely to rip off her propellor. She edged clear and then turned back towards the land as though her steering gear had given way. But before the blizzard closed down again, the Hallsands coastguard thought she was steaming out to sea.

Two hours later, the forecastle lookout on the *Marana* cried "Land dead ahead!" He was too late. We know from the account of one of the three survivors that Captain Higginson had kept his engines at full power for hours that afternoon in his efforts to clear the land. Now his engines drove him at full speed into the Blackstone Rock sticking up out of the sea almost under the Start lighthouse. She struck bow first, glanced off then her stern hit, tearing off her rudder and her propellor. Her engines stopped from the shock to the prop shaft and there she stuck broadside to the wind. Great waves washed over her. Suddenly there was a let up in the snow and the men of the Marana could see the Start Light which had been on all day because of the blizzard.

And the Start lighthouse saw them. At least Mrs.Briggs, wife of the Second Keeper saw them. She had seen the ship even before she struck, scraping by the rocks of the actual point below the light. She called Mr.Jones, the Head Keeper, and he just had time to see the *Marana* strike the Blackstone before the snow clamped down again. There was nothing he could do, except to send to Prawle for the rocket rescue apparatus, which he did, but he doubted if the man would get through to Prawle as the snow now filled every lane and gully.

On board *Marana*, it was clear that she was breaking up fast. But somehow the crew got the starboard lifeboat launched and as the port boat was jammed by the ship's list,22 men got into her. Most had lifebelts. Captain Higginson gave his to Anders Johnsen, an elderly Swedish fireman in the crew, who hadn't found one. Then the Captain, three mates, the Chief Engineer and a steward got the little jollyboat over the side and climbed in. Both boats got away from the ship. As they were whirled away to the west by the wind, the *Marana* broke in two. The stern sank on the eastern end of the rock, the bow section a little further to the west.

The jollyboat disappeared and was never seen again. The men in the large lifeboat did better, pulling with the wind along under the high cliffs. As they neared the shore a huge cross sea span the boat over. When the wave had passed only 12 were left close enough to cling to the upside-down boat's keel. Then another sea rolled the boat again. This time only four men survived. They managed to hang on until the boat was washed on to May Ledge in Horseley Cove were it was dashed to pieces. Amazingly, all four men managed to get ashore, but one, who had no seaboots, was severely cut about his feet. He was dragged and carried by the other three to the shelter of some trees.

After resting for a short while, it was clear that they would freeze to death unless they kept moving and so they stumbled upwards. But they did not get far before they sank exhausted under some bushes. Here they decided that the strongest of them should go on alone and bring help back.

The strongest of them was undoubtedly a Swede and he managed to reach Prawle Point coastguard station where he was given food and dry clothing. But he could not make himself understood. The coastguards realised he had come from a wreck and searched nearby, but it was five hours later before they heard weak cries and located the other three men. The injured man, another Swede called Ramosen, died as they arrived.

Unknown to them all, there had been another survivor from the lifeboat. He had reached the cliff-top, but fell exhausted and was soon covered by snow. His body was found nine days later, only 100 yards from the place the coastguards had reached the other three crewmen.

The Blackstone is divided in two and lies 300 yards south-south-east of Start Point and is really the northern end of the Cherrick Rocks, which dry at low tides and extend 200 yards further south. One peak of the Blackstone is nearest to the lighthouse. It is here that the *Marana*'s bow lies. After this peak there is a gap and the other two small peaks lie directly out to sea. This is where the remains of her stern lie. The rocks are often potted for crab.

Foot Note: Start Point runs a mile out to sea and takes its name from the Anglo-Saxon "steort" meaning a tail.

At one time there was a gallows on the tip of the Point and one execution recorded is that of September 28,1581, when Henri Muge, described as "a pirate" was hanged there in chains as a warning to the crews of other ships passing by.

Today Start Point Lighthouse is 203ft (62 metres) above sea level, though the height of the tower is just 91ft (28 metres). The 800,000 candlepower light flashes three times every ten seconds and has a range of 25 miles. In fog the siren sounds once every minute.

The South Devon coast path runs down the service road from the car park towards the lighthouse, which is now fully automatic. If you want to see the lighthouse, it is best to check with the car park attendant that it is open before you walk all the way down as the coast path branches off to the right.

65. DRYAD
Nestley Cove, 1891.

THE discovery that one of the bodies on the shore had a cork foot led to the positive identification of this wreck.

The *Dryad*, a 1035-ton fully-rigged iron barque of Liverpool, under command of Captain William Thomas, was out there in the blizzard of '91. She had left the Tyne on March 3 with a cargo for Valparaiso of coal, coke and mining equipment. Where she was when the hurricane caught her, no one knows as all 21 men aboard died in her wrecking just before midnight on the northern and steepest side of Start Point. At the time no one knew what ship she was, but the head lightkeeper Jones saw a ship's navigation lights in that position from the yard of his house beside the lighthouse. He and the other keepers went out to the cliff edge but could see nothing below them because of the blizzard.

It wasn't until the dawn that the bow of a ship could be seen amid the wreckage in a little cove by Nestley Point. And clinging to the slanting face of a rock, called "Jack Hatherly's Nose" by local fishermen, was the sole survivor.

He was not to survive for long. The rock to which he clung was about 100 yards from the wreck and only just clear of the surf. The man was scarcely conscious and could not hold a line, so Keeper Briggs went down the cliff on a rope. As he got close, the sailor lost his grip on the slippery rock and slid down under the next great wave.

What was left of the *Dryad* soon disappeared. An inquest was held in the London Inn, Hallsands, on March 15 when only two of eight bodies believed to be from the *Dryad* could be named.

The one which was first identified with certainty and which in turn led to the discovery of the name of the wreck was that of William Irvine, the 55-year-old ship's sailmaker from South Shields. He had a cork foot The other body identified later was that of a 17-year-old apprentice, Alfred Ford, of Hull, whose father came down to Devon to do so.

The inquest was told that a Tyne pilot who had been dropped off Beachy Head at 9 p.m on Monday, March 8, had warned Captain Thomas that his compass was several points out, and that the ship, launched in 1874, had a reputation for being a fast sailer. These points were made as though that might explain why the *Dryad* apparently still had some sails set when she hit the cliffs of Start, though it was clear that the blizzard was entirely to blame for her loss.

Foot Note: The body of William Irvine, "beloved husband of Annie", the man whose false foot identified the wreck as the *Dryad,* was buried at Stokenham. His headstone is easy to see in the graveyard there.

SECTION SIX –
Hallsands to Slapton.

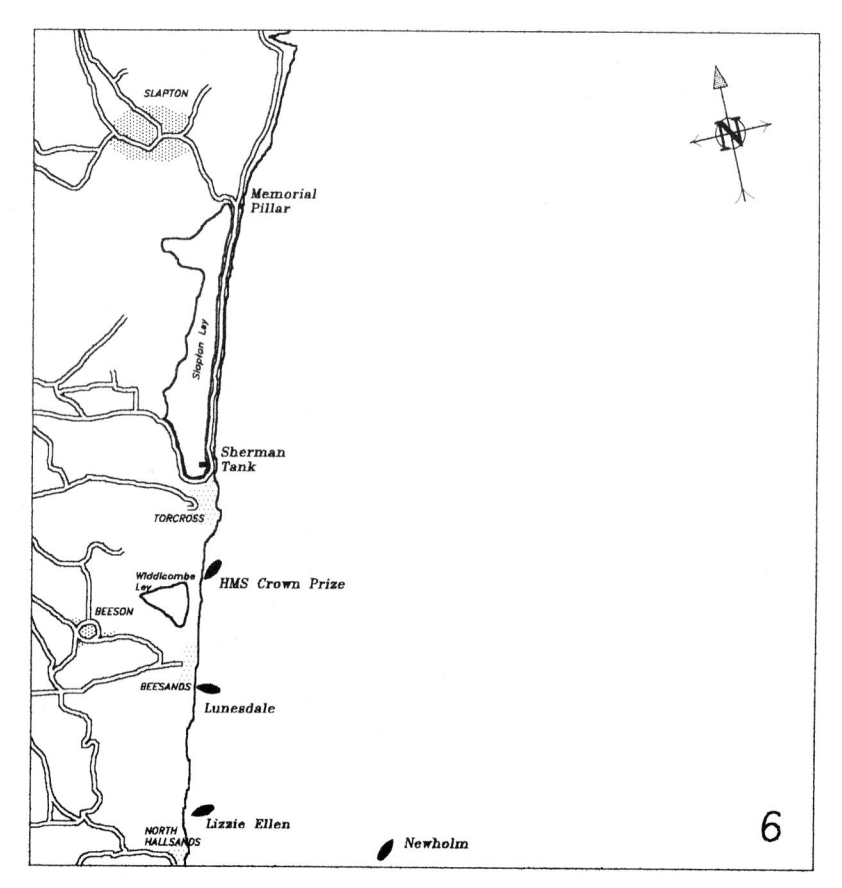

66. LIZZIE ELLEN.
Hallsands Cliff, 1891.

PRAWLE'S coastguards and rocket apparatus arrived at Beesands after the wagon which carried it had been stuck in snow several times. They got there at about 10pm on that terrible March 9, too late to help the *Lunesdale*. And they were in the wrong place to save all four crew of the 73-ton Chester schooner *Lizzie Ellen,* which went ashore at that time under the cliffs to the north of Hallsands.

The *Lizzie Ellen* was carrying a cargo of china clay from Charlestown, Cornwall to London, and had reached Portland Bill when the Force Ten wind from the east had beaten her back. Her master Robert Dodd had been forced to run before the wind and now crashed into the shore and broached to under the cliffs. Six fishermen from Hallsands climbed down to her. They were George Stone, Robert Trout, Thomas Trout (father of Ella; see *Newholm* No 68), James Lynn, William Mitchell and John Patey. With ropes they managed to rescue the Mate of the stricken ship, James Smith, and a sailor from Plymouth, Bob Clemens, but the ship's boy Francis Davies refused to jump into the sea and be hauled ashore. Captain Dodd stayed too long trying to persuade the terrified little lad, who kept crying for his mother. A moment or two later, the schooner broke up beneath them and the Captain and the boy were drowned. The six Hallsands fishermen received an R.N.L.I award for their bravery. The ship's dog escaped to shore and found a home in the village.

67. LUNESDALE.
Beesands. 1891.

THIS 141-ton three-masted schooner was another victim of the Great Blizzard of March 9, 1891. She had been bound from London to Runcorn with whiting (not the fish but fine chalk for use in polishing and whitewashing) and had been running blind before the storm since 11am when she was passing the Isle of Wight.

She struck the shore near Beesands village and giant waves swung her beam on. The crew and her captain, William Jones, were in the rigging when she struck, but no one could reach them.

A Beesands fisherman called John Roper rushed into the sea and hurled a conger line with a lead fishing weight tied on the end to Captain Jones. The lead weight went between Captain Jones's legs. He grabbed the conger line and then pulled a bigger rope attached to it aboard. The Captain tied the stout rope to a lifebuoy and called to one of the crew left on board to get hold of it. The man lost his grip.

Finally only Captain Jones was saved after holding on to the rope while jumping from the mizzen lee rigging near the stern. He was grabbed by Chief Officer Ridge of Torcross coastguard and others wading chest deep into the waves. Before the others in the rigging could be helped, they were washed away and drowned. So big were the seas that by the afternoon the whole schooner was flung up on the shore in pieces and left high and dry by the ebb tide. The wood from her was sold for £18.

68. NEWHOLM.
Off Hallsands. 1917.

THE sinking of the British steamer *Newholm* by a German mine only a mile from Hallsands on September 8, 1917, not only killed 20 men, but also created Britain's second "Grace Darling".

The area around Start Point was a favourite spot for the German mine-laying submarines of the Flanders Flotilla to set minefields to catch ships hugging the coast. At the beginning of September, Oberleutnant von Schrader in *UC-31* was busy doing just that. That night he put down six mines from the 18 in the dropping chutes of his 162 ft long boat and then took her down and away in the dark to repeat the process further up in the approaches to Dartmouth.

The *Newholm* at that time was crossing the Bay of Biscay on her way from Bilbao for Middlesbrough with a cargo of iron ore. Captain Magnus Smith of *Newholm* was given his Channel route instructions when he called at Brest as ordered. He said afterwards that they were all written in French and he didn't understand a word of them. It would not have saved his ship if he had, for he followed more or less the route set out in those papers.

At 11am on the fine clear morning of September 8, one of the mines laid by *UC-31* came into violent contact with the hull of the 3399-ton steamer, which was travelling at her top speed of ten knots. There was a huge explosion which ripped open holds one and two and she ploughed down by the bow almost instantly. She sank so fast that none of the crew had time to get to the boats and 20 of them went down with her. Nine men jumped overboard as she lurched away from underneath them. One of those men was Captain Smith. They all clung to floating wreckage and

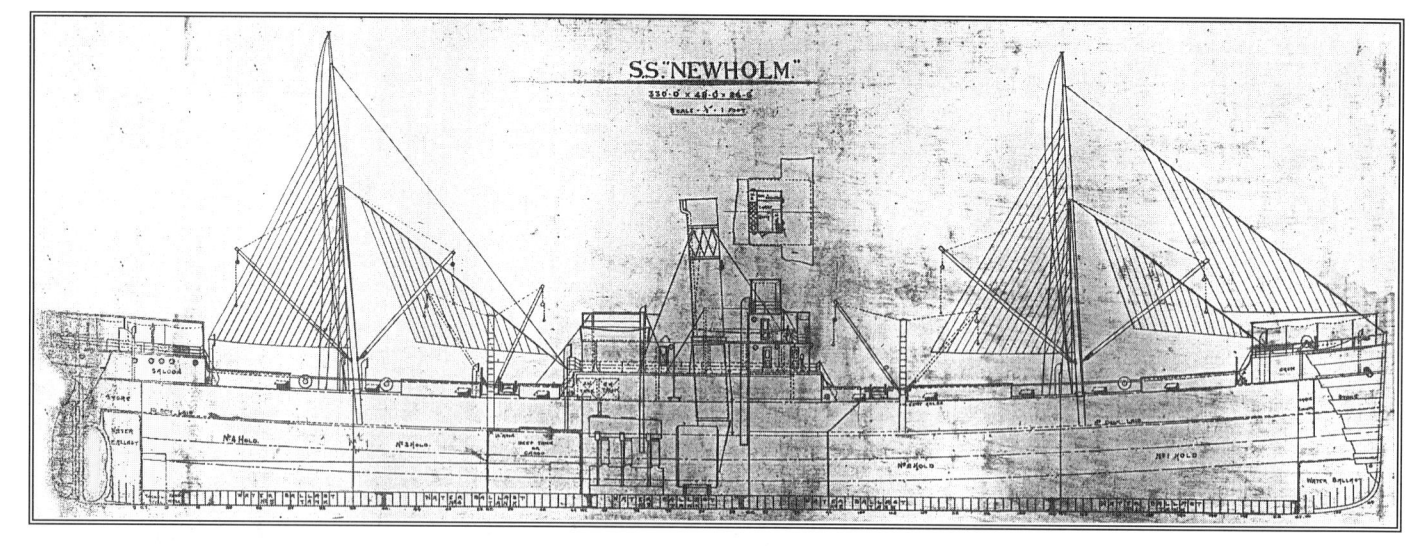

This part of the builder's plans show what the Newholm looked like.

hoped their sinking had been seen.

It had - by 20-year-old Ella Trout of Hallsands.

Ella had left school at 13 when her father died and had taken on the operation of his little fishing boat and his string of crab pots. Every day she went out to empty the pots and rebait them. She was in the middle of lifting the pots on that September morning when she heard the explosion and saw the *Newholm* disappear.

In the boat with her was her young cousin, ten-year-old William Trout. Without any hesitation Ella started rowing towards the floating wreckage. Rowing towards the scene too in another crabbing boat was William Stone of Frogmore. When they reached the spot, the crab boats picked up the nine survivors of the *Newholm*. When a naval patrol drifter, No.598 called *Direct Me*, reached them, the men were transferred into her and landed at Dartmouth.

The Admiralty were first to acknowledge Ella's efforts - they sent a letter of thanks to the man who actually owned the two crab boats, Mr.Spencer Fox, of The Gables, Salcombe, and enclosed £3 for William Stone and £1 for Ella Trout.

In 1918 Ella Trout was awarded the OBE in the New Year Honours List. It was announced in the Kingsbridge Gazette of January 11,1918: **"The King has been graciously pleased to confer the medal of the most excellent Order of the British Empire on Miss Ella Trout of Hallsands. This modern Grace Darling while fishing accompanied only by a boy of ten saw that a steamer had been torpedoed and was sinking. Though fully realising the danger she ran from the enemy submarine, she pulled with all her might to the wreck and succeeded in rescuing a drowning sailor"**

The story of Ella and the *Newholm* spread far and wide. All the other papers picked up the reference to Grace Darling, headlining their stories "Devon's Grace Darling" and comparing her with Grace Darling, the lighthouse keeper's daughter, who had rowed to the rescue of the *Forfarshire* survivors after that ship was sunk in the Farne Islands in 1838.

There were three Trout sisters, Ella, Patience and Edith and they had been made homeless earlier that year - on January 26,1917 - when a great storm with exceptionally high tides and a severe easterly gale wrecked Hallsands village. At midnight four houses collapsed when waves broke through the sea walls and washed away the foundations. Those built on the rocks were destroyed by giant waves. During a lull the villagers escaped to higher ground up the road, but after the morning's high tide only one of the 30 houses was still standing.

It is now almost certain that the removal of shingle from the beach in front of the villages of Beesands and Hallsands was to blame for the Hallsands disaster. Before the dredging Hallsands was protected by 60 feet of shingle above high water. After the removal of 650,000 tons of shingle - to make concrete for extensions to Devonport Dockyard - the beach level dropped so far that waves came right up to the sea walls. Storms which followed seriously damaged those wall, but it wasn't until angry fishermen refused to let the dredger moor to the shore in 1902 that the shingle removal stopped. But the damage was done and in 1903-4, the village was hit by storm waves, one of which destroyed the London Inn. It was the big storm of 1917, however, which was the final blow.

Foot Note: It took until 1924 for some of the villagers to be given new cottages at North Hallsands (locally called New Hallsands). But the rescue of the men of the *Newholm*, however, eased things earlier than that for the Trout sisters, who had refused to be rehoused out of the area. The parents of one of the men they rescued gave Ella some money to thank her for saving their son and the Trout girls used the money to build a house of their own on the cliff above the ruined village. The girls made over 8,000 concrete blocks with their own hands and helped mixing cement for Blake Brothers, the builders. They called their new home "Prospect House".

You can see the foundation stone to this day on the right-hand side of the building. It is inscribed:" This Foundation Stone was laid by Patience and Ella Trout O.B.E. on December 22nd 1923".

Seven years later they extended the building and renamed it "Trouts Hotel" with room for 66 guests. The hotel was a great success and many of their clients came back year after year. However, Ella died when she was 55 while visiting the graves of her father and that of Patience who had died three years earlier. Edith died in 1975. The hotel is now "Trouts Holiday Appartments" and is very popular, perched as it is on the cliff just above the ruined village. A special path leads from it down to the ruins.

It is interesting to note that Hallsands was the second village in the area to be destroyed by the sea. Strete Undercliffe, near Strete Gate and five miles north of Hallsands, is said to have been "engulfed by the Great Storm of 1703".

Today the *Newholm* lies with her back broken down the side of a huge sandbank less than a mile from Start Point in 145 feet of water.

69. HMS CROWN PRIZE.
The Cellars, Beesands, 1692.

UNTIL very recently this 26-gun man o'war was believed to have been lost near Dartmouth, but the discovery by divers of cannon marked with the Royal Navy's broad arrow has shown where she really lies - almost directly in front of the old slate quarry and lime kiln at the northern end of Beesands beach.

The 223-ton 85-feet-long *Crown Prize* was captured from the French in 1691 and became part of the English Navy She was anchored off Dartmouth on February 7, 1692, when a huge wind came up from the south-east. The seas rose so quickly that it was impossible for her to seek shelter in the Dart.

She fired guns as distress signals, but there was no way any boat could get out to her from the harbour whose narrow entrance was soon swept by massive waves. The next day the wind increased and Captain William Tichborn ordered his crew to cut the anchor cables and tried to beat out to sea. They had not got far when the wind swung to the east. For most of that night he tried to get out of Start Bay by rounding Start Point, but was trapped off the lee shore and driven back by the wind.

In the early hours of February 9 she was driven on shore.

Captain Tichborn and 21 of the crew died in the wrecking, though over 100 men are believed to have been saved.

Foot Note: The area by the quarry is known as Beesands Cellars, though the cellars, cut in the rock and used for salting and storing fish, have mostly disappeared Today there are a few cottages there just in front of the cliffs. Behind the village green - once a large caravan site - is Widdicombe Ley, a freshwater lake like its bigger counterpart at Slapton. The Beesands fisherman once used its fringing osiers for making crab pots.

The discovery of more cannon a few hundred yards directly out to sea from the Beesands pub, The Cricket Inn, does not mean another wreck there. As these cannon, like the ones at the Cellars, are iron six-pounders, cast near Uppsala in Sweden between 1670 and 1690, they are probably from the *Crown Prize* as well. During that period Sweden was the centre of the arms trade and supplied cannon to most of Europe.

70. SHERMAN TANK. Slapton, 1944.

TO call an American Army tank a shipwreck may seem odd, but in this case it is true!

The Sherman tank that sits at the village end of the car park at Torcross was once a "ship" - that is it was an amphibious tank, which was due to storm the Normandy beaches on D-day, but sank during a practice for that event. It is now a war memorial to 638 American soldiers and sailors who were killed by German E-boats at sea while training for the Normandy landings.

This area of the South Hams was evacuated of all civilians at the end of 1943, so that it could be used for live ammunition assault exercises by American forces practising for the storming of Utah Beach in Normandy. Though neither the troops nor the civilians knew it "Exercise Tiger" was held at Slapton and Torcross because the countryside bore some similarity to the Normandy coast.

The tank was one belonging to the U.S.70th Tank Battalion and was commanded by Orris Johnson. He was in charge of the rear tank of two being brought inshore in a tank landing craft. In this exercise all went well until the tank ahead of him went into reverse instead of forward gear at the launch and banged violently into Johnson's tank before getting it right and driving out of the open door of the landing ship and motoring successfully through the sea to the beach. It was then Johnson's turn. He launched all right, but only got some 15 feet before sinking like a stone. Even so all the crew got out safely and swam

Orris Johnson's tank, which sank off Slapton, is now a memorial to all the American servicemen who died in Exercise Tiger.

LST 289 managed to reach Dartmouth despite this damage during the battle with German E-boats on April 28, 1944.

back to the tank landing craft. Johnson believed for many years that the first tank by reversing into him had damaged the floatation collar, which was raised around the tank to turn it into a sort of boat.

For 30 years the tank rested upright on the seabed. The only people to see it were local divers. In my diving logbook I described it as "sitting on the seabed with all the hatches open as though the crew had popped out for a smoke". It was the home of some very large congers which had been fed by a keen underwater cameraman for a film and for ages afterwards would stick enormous heads out of the hatches at the mere sound of a diver's approach!

In 1984 the tank was raised due to the persistence of local hotelier Ken Small and became the memorial to the American servicemen who died when their small convoy of tank landing ships, taking part in Exercise Tiger, were discovered by accident by German E-boats, motor torpedo boats, operating out of Cherbourg, during the early hours of April 28,1944. The Germans sank two ships and damaged others; 638 Americans died. In the real assault on June 6,1944, on Utah Beach, for which Exercise Tiger had been just a practice,12 Americans died and 100 were wounded.

Foot Note: Only after the tank was raised did they find that the reason that Orris Johnson's tank sank so quickly was not damage to the floatation collar, but the fact that a watertight plate underneath the engine was missing, presumably not replaced after maintenance, leaving a hole in the bottom!

A granite pillar, flanked by flagpoles, further along Slapton Sands was erected by the U.S.Army to thank the local inhabitants for their sacrifice in leaving their homes for this live-ammo training.

SECTION SEVEN – Strete Gate to Dartmouth

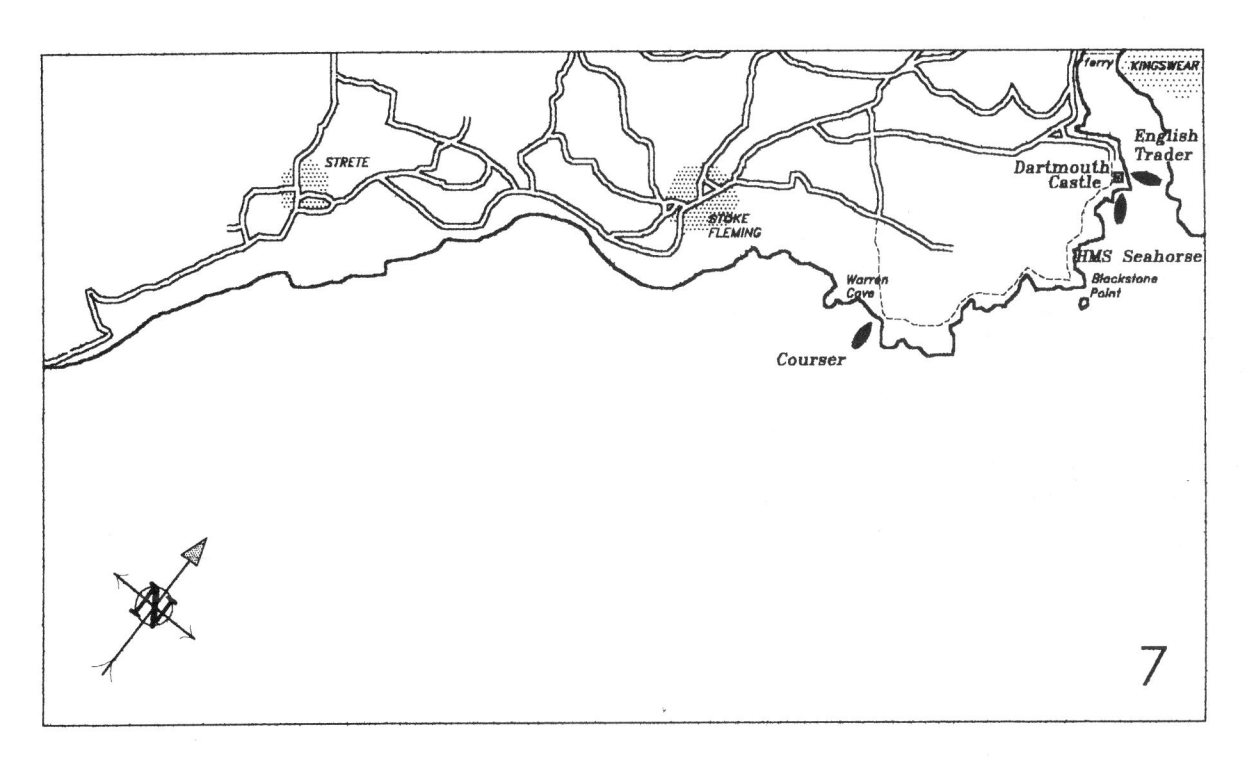

Though the path goes inland from Strete Gate at the end of Slapton Sands, it returns to the sea coast at Warren Cove before following the cliffs to Dartmouth. The wreck of the *Courser* lies close to the spot where the path rejoins the sea.

71. COURSER.
Warren Cove, 1870.

WHILE heading for Torbay for orders from Fecamp, France, this Brixham schooner ran into the mother and father of easterly gales while crossing the Channel. She was in ballast and during the Saturday night lost her mainsail to the wind. On Sunday morning, February 13, 1870, she was seen off Blackstone Point near Dartmouth Castle at anchor and flying a signal of distress - her ensign upside down.

She was assumed to be unmanageable, and when her anchors dragged at about 9 a.m., it was clear that she was. The Dartmouth harbour tug *Guide* set off to help her. But the steam tug was not quick enough and before she could catch up with the schooner she was almost on the rocks of Warren Point.

The captain of *Guide* tried to put his ship between her and the rocks, but she was too close. How close is demonstrated by the odd action of Captain Brusey of *Courser* - he threw his "opera glass" on the rocks where it was picked up by one of the onlookers who had now started to gather in great numbers.

Soon the schooner struck. As she did, she started to break up and Captain Brusey and his five crew took to their boat. They then started to row towards the tug. The people on the rocks shouted to them to go back to their ship as the *Guide* would be able to take them off from there more easily. Even if they heard it, the men in the boat ignored the advice and continued to pull towards the tug.

They were so cold and the wind so strong that they made little headway. Just as the tug reached them, a huge wave welled up and turned the boat over. Lifebuoys were thrown to them from the tug, but only one man managed to grab one. The rest drowned in full view of hundreds of people who crowded the rocks and cliffs.

The man who did catch a lifebuoy nearly died too. He managed to reach the rocks, but if it hadn't been for the bravery of a Dartmouth man, described by the Dartmouth Chronicle as "Mr.Coaker, brother to the landlord of the Royal Oak", he would have been washed away. Mr.Coaker "at the imminent risk of his own life ventured out and grasping the seaman by his clothes managed to bring him safely in and with the help of restoratives he soon recovered".

This was the second loss of a sailing ship close to Dartmouth within a week. The earlier wreck was that of the *Eureka*, a brig from Newcastle to Plymouth on Froward Point at the other side of the harbour entrance. Three of her crew of nine were lost.

At the inquest on the *Courser's* victims, it was stressed several times that Dartmouth had no lifeboat and no rocket apparatus, despite the fact that it was an important port of refuge as well as a port of call.

All of the *Courser's* crew could have been saved, the inquest jury were told, if a breeches buoy and rocket apparatus had been available. The inquest was held at the Strike's Sun Inn, and the packed room was totally silent as the survivor of the schooner, William Lowton, aged 19, an able seaman, told how they lost their mainsail in mid-Channel. They ran for shelter to Dartmouth. He criticised the tug boat for not coming closer to save them. They were only three yards from the shore when the boat capsized and everyone on the rocks had done their best to help them. "I was the only one saved".

A juror pointed out that the tug had done her best and couldn't have got any closer without wrecking herself. The chief officer of the coastguard said that a rocket apparatus could have been used to save the men.

At the end of the evidence, the jury found the men were "accidentally drowned", but also signed a petition to the National Lifeboat Institution asking for a lifeboat to be placed in Dartmouth. However, it was six years later that a public meeting in the town sent another petition to the Lifeboat Institution in July,1876, and finally got a lifeboat in 1878.

72. ENGLISH TRADER
Dartmouth Castle, 1937.

THERE are cannon underwater at the mouth of the Dart, but there is no evidence to show that they were ship-borne victims of the guns of Dartmouth Castle. They may have been deliberately dumped from the battlements during the centuries since the castle was built in 1481 when it was one of the first designed to take cannon.

At first it had seven guns covering a 750-foot chain supported by small boats, which was fastened across the estuary in times of trouble. Kingswear Castle on the other side was abandoned as a fort when cannon became powerful enough to cover the entrance from one side only.

However, the 14-gun HMS *Seahorse* was lost just below the the Castle walls on December 26, 1711, and the guns could be from her wreck.

The *English Trader* was wrecked right over those cannon and close underneath the walls of Dartmouth Castle in the dawn of January 23,1937.

The English Trader was pinned by her nose beside Dartmouth Castle

She was one of the first examples of the art of salvaging a ship by cutting her half. The *English Trader* was a London-registered steamer. She came up the Channel in January, 1937, loaded with grain from San Nicholas, near Buenos Aires in the Argentine, and was heading for the Baltic. But first she had to put into Dartmouth to pick up more coal for her bunkers.

In the dawn of January 23, she was just about to enter Dartmouth when her steering gear failed. Her captain shut down her engines and she drifted on to the Check Stone, the rock which can be seen on the west side of Castle Cove under the castle walls.

First on the scene was the Royal Navy's 1350-ton destroyer, *HMS Witch*, which laid out anchors and held the steamer's stern by sheer engine power from swinging round on to the rocks. Then the next rescuers, the big Admiralty tug *Retort* and the Dutch salvage tugs *Witte Zee* and *Zwarte Zee*, which had been waiting for work in Dartmouth, took up hawsers and when the tide rose in the afternoon took the strain. But even their combined horsepower failed to shift the ship.

The next plan was to shift the grain out of her into

lighters, but the weather was growing worse and the lighters could not get alongside. Now it became clear that the *English Trader* was firmly pinned by her nose to the rocks and the tide instead of lifting her started to flow over her bow.

That and a gale forecast with the wind already strengthening brought the Torbay lifeboat to the stricken steamer. She stood by all day and was then asked to stand by during the following night. There were 52 men on board the *English Trader* and there was no way they could get ashore through the huge seas.

The gale came as predicted from the South-South-East and great walls of foam boiled through the harbour entrance. At six in the morning the captain of the *Trader* believed all was lost. He ordered distress rockets to be fired. His ship was now completely broadside to the Castle and pounding so heavily that it was all he and his men could do to stay on their feet. Though her bow was pointing out to sea, the waves found it no obstacle and smashed the port side of the bridge before racing on to flood the holds further aft.

When he saw the distress rockets, Coxswain William Mogridge of the Torbay lifeboat, the *George Shee*, earned a clasp to his bronze medal, by taking the boat in between the steamer and the shore to get some shelter from the wind. As each wave burst the teeth of rocks appeared all around the lifeboat, which was now rising and falling 15 feet up the steamer's side. It took them 20 minutes to get into position and then she was held there by bursts of ahead and astern on her engines.

A rope ladder was flung over the steamer's side and the 52 men hurtled down into the lifeboat. Only 32 of them were crew of the *English Trader*. The rest were 15 stevedores, three salvage officers, a pilot and a navy signalman, all of whom had been put aboard during the early salvage efforts.

Getting in between the ship and the shore had been child's play compared with the difficulty of getting out. The lifeboat was heavily laden now and the cox'n had to back out under the stern into a trough of a wave and then once clear of the hull and out in the wind, open up his engines and give her full speed ahead. It worked and the lifeboat got safely back into Dartmouth after 31 hours on duty.

When the wind stopped, the *English Trader* was still there and still held fast by the rocks. The salvage men decided there was only one thing to do - cut her free from her bows and tow the undamaged section to Southampton where a new bow could be fitted. Cutting the aft section away from the bow took three weeks, but four months later the second *English Trader* was complete and back in service while the bows of the original stayed stuck on the rocks of Castle Cove for weeks afterwards before being taken away for scrap.